Travel phrasebooks collection
«Everything Will Be Okay!»

T&P Books Publishing

PHRASEBOOK

— ITALIAN —

I0005794

By Andrey Taranov

THE MOST IMPORTANT PHRASES

This phrasebook contains the most important phrases and questions for basic communication
Everything you need to survive overseas

T&P BOOKS

Phrasebook + 3000-word dictionary

English-Italian phrasebook & topical vocabulary

By Andrey Taranov

The collection of "Everything Will Be Okay" travel phrasebooks published by T&P Books is designed for people traveling abroad for tourism and business. The phrasebooks contain what matters most - the essentials for basic communication. This is an indispensable set of phrases to "survive" while abroad.

This book also includes a small topical vocabulary that contains roughly 3,000 of the most frequently used words. Another section of the phrasebook provides a gastronomical dictionary that may help you order food at a restaurant or buy groceries at the store.

T&P Books Publishing
www.tpbooks.com

ISBN: 978-1-78492-430-0

This book is also available in E-book formats.
Please visit www.tpbooks.com or the major online bookstores.

FOREWORD

The collection of "Everything Will Be Okay" travel phrasebooks published by T&P Books is designed for people traveling abroad for tourism and business. The phrasebooks contain what matters most - the essentials for basic communication. This is an indispensable set of phrases to "survive" while abroad.

This phrasebook will help you in most cases where you need to ask something, get directions, find out how much something costs, etc. It can also resolve difficult communication situations where gestures just won't help.

This book contains a lot of phrases that have been grouped according to the most relevant topics. The edition also includes a small vocabulary that contains roughly 3,000 of the most frequently used words. Another section of the phrasebook provides a gastronomical dictionary that may help you order food at a restaurant or buy groceries at the store.

Take "Everything Will Be Okay" phrasebook with you on the road and you'll have an irreplaceable traveling companion who will help you find your way out of any situation and teach you to not fear speaking with foreigners.

TABLE OF CONTENTS

T&P Books Publishing

PRONUNCIATION

T&P phonetic alphabet	Italian example	English example
[a]	casco ['kasko]	shorter than in ask
[e]	sfera ['sfera]	elm, medal
[i]	filo ['filo]	shorter than in feet
[o]	dolce ['doltʃe]	pod, John
[u]	siluro [si'luro]	book
[y]	würstel ['vyrstel]	fuel, tuna
[b]	busta ['busta]	baby, book
[d]	andare [an'dare]	day, doctor
[ʣ]	zinco ['ʣinko]	beads, kids
[ʤ]	Norvegia [nor'veʤa]	joke, general
[ʒ]	garage [ga'raʒ]	forge, pleasure
[f]	ferrovia [ferro'via]	face, food
[g]	ago ['ago]	game, gold
[k]	cocktail ['koktejl]	clock, kiss
[j]	piazza ['pjattsa]	yes, New York
[l]	olive [o'live]	lace, people
[ʎ]	figlio ['fiʎʎo]	daily, million
[m]	mosaico [mo'zaiko]	magic, milk
[n]	treno ['treno]	name, normal
[ŋ]	granchio ['graŋkio]	English, ring
[ɲ]	magnete [ma'ɲete]	canyon, new
[p]	pallone [pal'lone]	pencil, private
[r]	futuro [fu'turo]	rice, radio
[s]	triste ['triste]	city, boss
[ʃ]	piscina [pi'ʃina]	machine, shark
[t]	estintore [estin'tore]	tourist, trip
[ts]	spezie ['spetsie]	cats, tsetse fly
[tʃ]	lancia ['lantʃa]	church, French
[v]	volo ['volo]	very, river
[w]	whisky ['wiski]	vase, winter
[z]	deserto [de'zerto]	zebra, please

LIST OF ABBREVIATIONS

English abbreviations

ab.	-	about
adj	-	adjective
adv	-	adverb
anim.	-	animate
as adj	-	attributive noun used as adjective
e.g.	-	for example
etc.	-	et cetera
fam.	-	familiar
fem.	-	feminine
form.	-	formal
inanim.	-	inanimate
masc.	-	masculine
math	-	mathematics
mil.	-	military
n	-	noun
pl	-	plural
pron.	-	pronoun
sb	-	somebody
sing.	-	singular
sth	-	something
v aux	-	auxiliary verb
vi	-	intransitive verb
vi, vt	-	intransitive, transitive verb
vt	-	transitive verb

Italian abbreviations

agg	-	adjective
f	-	feminine noun
f pl	-	feminine plural
m	-	masculine noun
m pl	-	masculine plural
m, f	-	masculine, feminine
pl	-	plural
v aus	-	auxiliary verb
vi	-	intransitive verb

vi, vt	-	intransitive, transitive verb
vr	-	reflexive verb
vt	-	transitive verb

T&P BOOKS

ITALIAN PHRASEBOOK

This section contains
important phrases that may
come in handy in various
real-life situations.
The phrasebook will help
you ask for directions, clarify
a price, buy tickets, and
order food at a restaurant

T&P Books Publishing

PHRASEBOOK
CONTENTS

T&P Books Publishing

The bare minimum

Excuse me, ...	**Mi scusi, ...** [mi 'skuzi, ...]
Hello.	**Buongiorno.** [buon'dʒorno]
Thank you.	**Grazie.** [gratsie]
Good bye.	**Arrivederci.** [arrive'dertʃi]
Yes.	**Sì.** [si]
No.	**No.** [no]
I don't know.	**Non lo so.** [non lo so]
Where? | Where to? | When?	**Dove? | Dove? | Quando?** [dove? | 'dove? | 'kwando?]

I need ...	**Ho bisogno di ...** [o bi'zoɲo di ...]
I want ...	**Voglio ...** [voʎʎo ...]
Do you have ...?	**Avete ...?** [a'vete ...?]
Is there a ... here?	**C'è un /una/ ... qui?** [tʃe un /'una/ ... kwi?]
May I ...?	**Posso ...?** [posso ...?]
..., please (polite request)	**per favore** [per fa'vore]

I'm looking for ...	**Sto cercando ...** [sto tʃer'kando ...]
the restroom	**bagno** [baɲo]
an ATM	**bancomat** [bankomat]
a pharmacy (drugstore)	**farmacia** [farma'tʃija]
a hospital	**ospedale** [ospe'dale]
the police station	**stazione di polizia** [sta'tsjone di poli'tsia]
the subway	**metropolitana** [metropoli'tana]

a taxi	**taxi**
	['taksi]
the train station	**stazione**
	[sta'tsjone]

My name is ...	**Mi chiamo ...**
	[mi 'kjamo ...]
What's your name?	**Come si chiama?**
	[kome si 'kjama?]
Could you please help me?	**Mi può aiutare, per favore?**
	[mi pu'o aju'tare, per fa'vore?]
I've got a problem.	**Ho un problema.**
	[o un pro'blema]
I don't feel well.	**Mi sento male.**
	[mi 'sento 'male]
Call an ambulance!	**Chiamate l'ambulanza!**
	[kja'mate lambu'lantsa!]
May I make a call?	**Posso fare una telefonata?**
	[posso 'fare 'una telefo'nata?]

I'm sorry.	**Mi dispiace.**
	[mi dis'pjatʃe]
You're welcome.	**Prego.**
	[prego]

I, me	**io**
	[io]
you (inform.)	**tu**
	[tu]
he	**lui**
	[lui]
she	**lei**
	['lei]
they (masc.)	**loro**
	[loro]
they (fem.)	**loro**
	[loro]
we	**noi**
	[noi]
you (pl)	**voi**
	[voi]
you (sg, form.)	**Lei**
	['lei]

ENTRANCE	**ENTRATA**
	[en'trata]
EXIT	**USCITA**
	[u'ʃita]
OUT OF ORDER	**FUORI SERVIZIO**
	[fu'ori ser'vitsio]
CLOSED	**CHIUSO**
	[kjuzo]

OPEN	**APERTO** [a'perto]
FOR WOMEN	**DONNE** [donne]
FOR MEN	**UOMINI** [u'omini]

Questions

Where?

Dove?
[dove?]

Where to?

Dove?
[dove?]

Where from?

Da dove?
[da 'dove?]

Why?

Perché?
[per'ke?]

For what reason?

Perché?
[per'ke?]

When?

Quando?
[kwando?]

How long?

Per quanto tempo?
[per 'kwanto 'tempo?]

At what time?

A che ora?
[a ke 'ora?]

How much?

Quanto?
[kwanto?]

Do you have ...?

Avete ...?
[a'vete ...?]

Where is ...?

Dov'è ...?
[dov'e ...?]

What time is it?

Che ore sono?
[ke 'ore 'sono?]

May I make a call?

Posso fare una telefonata?
[posso 'fare 'una telefo'nata?]

Who's there?

Chi è?
[ki 'e?]

Can I smoke here?

Si può fumare qui?
[si pu'o fu'mare kwi?]

May I ...?

Posso ...?
[posso ...?]

Needs

I'd like ...	**Vorrei ...** [vor'rej ...]
I don't want ...	**Non voglio ...** [non 'voλλo ...]
I'm thirsty.	**Ho sete.** [o 'sete]
I want to sleep.	**Ho sonno.** [o 'sonno]
I want ...	**Voglio ...** [voλλo ...]
to wash up	**lavarmi** [la'varmi]
to brush my teeth	**lavare i denti** [la'vare i 'denti]
to rest a while	**riposae un po'** [ripo'zae un 'po]
to change my clothes	**cambiare i vestiti** [kam'bjare i ve'stiti]
to go back to the hotel	**tornare in albergo** [tor'nare in al'bergo]
to buy ...	**comprare ...** [kom'prare ...]
to go to ...	**andare a ...** [an'dare a ...]
to visit ...	**visitare ...** [vizi'tare ...]
to meet with ...	**incontrare ...** [inkon'trare ...]
to make a call	**fare una telefonata** [fare 'una telefo'nata]
I'm tired.	**Sono stanco /stanca/.** [sono 'stanko /'stanka/]
We are tired.	**Siamo stanchi.** [sjamo 'staŋki]
I'm cold.	**Ho freddo.** [o 'freddo]
I'm hot.	**Ho caldo.** [o 'kaldo]
I'm OK.	**Sto bene.** [sto 'bene]

I need to make a call.	**Devo fare una telefonata.**
	[devo 'fare 'una telefo'nata]
I need to go to the restroom.	**Devo andare in bagno.**
	[devo an'dare in 'baɲo]
I have to go.	**Devo andare.**
	[devo an'dare]
I have to go now.	**Devo andare adesso.**
	[devo an'dare a'desso]

Asking for directions

Excuse me, ...	**Mi scusi, ...** [mi 'skuzi, ...]
Where is ...?	**Dove si trova ...?** [dove si 'trova ...?]
Which way is ...?	**Da che parte è ...?** [da ke 'parte e ...?]
Could you help me, please?	**Mi può aiutare, per favore?** [mi pu'o aju'tare, per fa'vore?]
I'm looking for ...	**Sto cercando ...** [sto tʃer'kando ...]
I'm looking for the exit.	**Sto cercando l'uscita.** [sto tʃer'kando lu'ʃita]
I'm going to ...	**Sto andando a ...** [sto an'dando a ...]
Am I going the right way to ...?	**Sto andando nella direzione giusta per ...?** [sto an'dando 'nella dire'tsjone 'dʒusta per ...?]
Is it far?	**E' lontano?** [e lon'tano?]
Can I get there on foot?	**Posso andarci a piedi?** [posso an'darsi a 'pjedi?]
Can you show me on the map?	**Può mostrarmi sulla piantina?** [pu'o mo'strarmi 'sulla pjan'tina?]
Show me where we are right now.	**Può mostrarmi dove ci troviamo?** [puo mo'strarmi 'dove tʃi tro'vjamo]
Here	**Qui** [kwi]
There	**Là** [la]
This way	**Da questa parte** [da 'kwesto 'parte]
Turn right.	**Giri a destra.** [dʒiri a 'destra]
Turn left.	**Giri a sinistra.** ['dʒiri a si'nistra]

first (second, third) turn	**La prima (la seconda, la terza) strada** [la 'prima (la se'konda, la 'tertsa) 'strada]
to the right	**a destra** [a 'destra]
to the left	**a sinistra** [a si'nistra]
Go straight ahead.	**Vada sempre dritto.** [vada 'sempre 'dritto]

Signs

WELCOME!	**BENVENUTO!** [benve'nuto!]
ENTRANCE	**ENTRATA** [en'trata]
EXIT	**USCITA** [u'ʃita]
PUSH	**SPINGERE** [spindʒere]
PULL	**TIRARE** [ti'rare]
OPEN	**APERTO** [a'perto]
CLOSED	**CHIUSO** [kjuzo]
FOR WOMEN	**DONNE** [donne]
FOR MEN	**UOMINI** [u'omini]
GENTLEMEN, GENTS	**BAGNO UOMINI** [baɲo u'omini]
WOMEN	**BAGNO DONNE** [baɲo 'donne]
DISCOUNTS	**SCONTI** [skonti]
SALE	**IN SALDO** [saldi]
FREE	**GRATIS** ['gratis]
NEW!	**NOVITÀ!** [novi'ta!]
ATTENTION!	**ATTENZIONE!** [atten'tsjone!]
NO VACANCIES	**COMPLETO** [kom'pleto]
RESERVED	**RISERVATO** [rizer'vato]
ADMINISTRATION	**AMMINISTRAZIONE** [amministra'tsjone]
STAFF ONLY	**RISERVATO AL PERSONALE** [rizer'vato al perso'nale]

BEWARE OF THE DOG!	**ATTENTI AL CANE!** [at'tenti al 'kane]
NO SMOKING!	**VIETATO FUMARE** [vje'tato fu'mare]
DO NOT TOUCH!	**NON TOCCARE** [non tok'kare]
DANGEROUS	**PERICOLOSO** [periko'lozo]
DANGER	**PERICOLO** [pe'rikolo]
HIGH VOLTAGE	**ALTA TENSIONE** [alta ten'sjone]
NO SWIMMING!	**DIVIETO DI BALNEAZIONE** [di'vjeto di balnea'tsjone]
OUT OF ORDER	**FUORI SERVIZIO** [fu'ori ser'vitsio]
FLAMMABLE	**INFIAMMABILE** [infjam'mabile]
FORBIDDEN	**VIETATO** [vje'tato]
NO TRESPASSING!	**VIETATO L'ACCESSO** [vje'tato la'tʃesso]
WET PAINT	**PITTURA FRESCA** [pitt'ura 'freska]
CLOSED FOR RENOVATIONS	**CHIUSO PER RESTAURO** [kjuzo per res'tauro]
WORKS AHEAD	**LAVORI IN CORSO** [la'vori in 'korso]
DETOUR	**DEVIAZIONE** [devia'tsjone]

Transportation. General phrases

plane	**aereo** [a'ereo]
train	**treno** [treno]
bus	**autobus** [autobus]
ferry	**traghetto** [tra'getto]
taxi	**taxi** ['taksi]
car	**macchina** ['makkina]

schedule	**orario** [o'rario]
Where can I see the schedule?	**Dove posso vedere l'orario?** [dove 'posso ve'dere lo'rario?]
workdays (weekdays)	**giorni feriali** [dʒorni fe'rjali]
weekends	**sabato e domenica** [sabato e do'menika]
holidays	**giorni festivi** [dʒorni fe'stivi]

DEPARTURE	**PARTENZA** [par'tentsa]
ARRIVAL	**ARRIVO** [ar'rivo]
DELAYED	**IN RITARDO** [in ri'tardo]
CANCELLED	**CANCELLATO** [kantʃelllato]

next (train, etc.)	**il prossimo** [il 'prossimo]
first	**il primo** [il 'primo]
last	**l'ultimo** [lultimo]

When is the next ...?	**Quando è il prossimo ...?** [kwando e il 'prossimo ...?]
When is the first ...?	**Quando è il primo ...?** [kwando e il 'primo ...?]

When is the last …?

Quando è l'ultimo …?
[kwando e 'lultimo …?]

transfer (change of trains, etc.)

scalo
[skalo]

to make a transfer

effettuare uno scalo
[efettu'are 'uno 'skalo]

Do I need to make a transfer?

Devo cambiare?
[devo kam'bjare?]

Buying tickets

Where can I buy tickets?	**Dove posso comprare i biglietti?** [dove 'posso kom'prare i biʎ'ʎeti?]
ticket	**biglietto** [biʎ'ʎetto]
to buy a ticket	**comprare un biglietto** [kom'prare un biʎ'ʎetto]
ticket price	**il prezzo del biglietto** [il 'prettso del biʎ'ʎetto]

Where to?	**Dove?** [dove?]
To what station?	**In quale stazione?** [in 'kwale sta'tsjone?]
I need ...	**Avrei bisogno di ...** [av'rej bi'zoɲo di ...]
one ticket	**un biglietto** [un biʎ'ʎetto]
two tickets	**due biglietti** [due biʎ'ʎeti]
three tickets	**tre biglietti** [tre biʎ'ʎeti]

one-way	**solo andata** [solo an'data]
round-trip	**andata e ritorno** [an'data e ri'torno]
first class	**prima classe** [prima 'klasse]
second class	**seconda classe** [se'konda 'klasse]

today	**oggi** [odʒi]
tomorrow	**domani** [do'mani]
the day after tomorrow	**dopodomani** [dopodo'mani]
in the morning	**la mattina** [la mat'tina]
in the afternoon	**nel pomeriggio** [nel pome'ridʒo]
in the evening	**la sera** [la 'sera]

aisle seat

posto lato corridoio
[posto 'lato korri'dojo]

window seat

posto lato finestrino
[posto 'lato fine'strino]

How much?

Quanto?
[kwanto?]

Can I pay by credit card?

Posso pagare con la carta di credito?
[posso pa'gare kon la 'karta di 'kredito?]

Bus

bus	**autobus** [autobus]
intercity bus	**autobus interurbano** [autobus interur'bano]
bus stop	**fermata dell'autobus** [fer'mata dell 'autobus]
Where's the nearest bus stop?	**Dov'è la fermata dell'autobus più vicina?** [dov'e la fer'mata dell 'autobus pju vi'tʃina?]
number (bus ~, etc.)	**numero** [numero]
Which bus do I take to get to ...?	**Quale autobus devo prendere per andare a ...?** [kwale 'autobus 'devo 'prendere per an'dare a ...?]
Does this bus go to ...?	**Questo autobus va a ...?** [kwesto 'autobus va a ...?]
How frequent are the buses?	**Qual'è la frequenza delle corse degli autobus?** [kwal e la fre'kwentsa 'delle 'korse 'deʎʎi 'autobus?]
every 15 minutes	**ogni quindici minuti** [oɲi 'kwinditʃi mi'nuti]
every half hour	**ogni mezzora** [oɲi med'dzora]
every hour	**ogni ora** [oɲi 'ora]
several times a day	**più a volte al giorno** [pju a 'volte al 'dʒorno]
... times a day	**... volte al giorno** [... 'volte al 'dʒorno]
schedule	**orario** [o'rario]
Where can I see the schedule?	**Dove posso vedere l'orario?** [dove 'posso ve'dere lo'rario?]
When is the next bus?	**Quando passa il prossimo autobus?** [kwando 'passa il 'prossimo 'autobus?]
When is the first bus?	**A che ora è il primo autobus?** [a ke 'ora e il 'primo 'autobus?]
When is the last bus?	**A che ora è l'ultimo autobus?** [a ke 'ora e 'lultimo 'autobus?]

stop	**fermata** [fer'mata]
next stop	**prossima fermata** [prossima fer'mata]
last stop (terminus)	**ultima fermata** [ultima fer'mata]
Stop here, please.	**Può fermarsi qui, per favore.** [pu'o fer'marsi kwi, per fa'vore]
Excuse me, this is my stop.	**Mi scusi, questa è la mia fermata.** [mi 'skuzi, 'kwesta e la 'mia fer'mata]

Train

train	**treno** [treno]
suburban train	**treno locale** [treno lo'kale]
long-distance train	**treno a lunga percorrenza** [treno a 'lunga perkor'rentsa]
train station	**stazione** [sta'tsjone]
Excuse me, where is the exit to the platform?	**Mi scusi, dov'è l'uscita per il binario?** [mi 'skuzi, dov'e lu'ʃita per il binario?]

Does this train go to ...?	**Questo treno va a ...?** [kwesto 'treno va a ...?]
next train	**il prossimo treno** [il 'prossimo 'treno]
When is the next train?	**Quando è il prossimo treno?** [kwando e il 'prossimo 'treno?]
Where can I see the schedule?	**Dove posso vedere l'orario?** [dove 'posso ve'dere lo'rario?]
From which platform?	**Da quale binario?** [da 'kwale bi'nario?]
When does the train arrive in ...?	**Quando il treno arriva a ... ?** [kwando il 'treno ar'riva a ...?]

Please help me.	**Mi può aiutare, per favore.** [mi pu'o aju'tare, per fa'vore]
I'm looking for my seat.	**Sto cercando il mio posto.** [sto tʃer'kando il 'mio 'posto]
We're looking for our seats.	**Stiamo cercando i nostri posti.** [stjamo tʃer'kando i 'nostri 'posti]
My seat is taken.	**Il mio posto è occupato.** [il 'mio 'posto e okku'pato]
Our seats are taken.	**I nostri posti sono occupati.** [i 'nostri 'posti 'sono okku'pati]

I'm sorry but this is my seat.	**Mi scusi, ma questo è il mio posto.** [mi 'skwzi, ma 'kwesto e il 'mio 'posto]
Is this seat taken?	**E' occupato?** [e okku'pato?]
May I sit here?	**Posso sedermi qui?** [posso se'dermi kwi?]

On the train. Dialogue (No ticket)

Ticket, please.
Biglietto per favore.
[biʎ'ʎetto per fa'vore]

I don't have a ticket.
Non ho il biglietto.
[non 'o il biʎ'ʎetto]

I lost my ticket.
Ho perso il biglietto.
[o 'perso il biʎ'ʎetto]

I forgot my ticket at home.
Ho dimenticato il biglietto a casa.
[o dimenti'kato il biʎ'ʎetto a 'kaza]

You can buy a ticket from me.
Può acquistare il biglietto da me.
[pu'o akwi'stare il biʎ'ʎetto da 'me]

You will also have to pay a fine.
Deve anche pagare una multa.
[deve 'aŋke pa'gare 'una 'multa]

Okay.
Va bene.
[va 'bene]

Where are you going?
Dove va?
[dove va?]

I'm going to …
Vado a …
[vado a …]

How much? I don't understand.
Quanto? Non capisco.
[kwanto? non ka'pisko]

Write it down, please.
Lo può scrivere, per favore?
[lo pu'o 'skrivere, per fa'vore]

Okay. Can I pay with a credit card?
D'accordo. Posso pagare con la carta di credito?
[dak'kordo. 'posso pa'gare kon la 'karta di 'kredito?]

Yes, you can.
Sì.
[si]

Here's your receipt.
Ecco la sua ricevuta.
[ekko la 'sua ritʃe'vuta]

Sorry about the fine.
Mi dispiace per la multa.
[mi dis'pjatʃe per la 'multa]

That's okay. It was my fault.
Va bene così. È stata colpa mia.
[va 'bene ko'si. e 'stata 'kolpa 'mia]

Enjoy your trip.
Buon viaggio.
[bu'on 'vjadʒo]

Taxi

taxi	**taxi** ['taksi]
taxi driver	**tassista** [tas'sista]
to catch a taxi	**prendere un taxi** [prendere un 'taksi]
taxi stand	**posteggio taxi** [pos'tedʒo 'taksi]
Where can I get a taxi?	**Dove posso prendere un taxi?** [dove 'posso 'prendere un 'taksi?]

to call a taxi	**chiamare un taxi** [kja'mare un 'taksi]
I need a taxi.	**Ho bisogno di un taxi.** [o bi'zoɲo di un 'taksi]
Right now.	**Adesso.** [a'desso]
What is your address (location)?	**Qual'è il suo indirizzo?** [kwal e il 'suo indi'rittso?]
My address is ...	**Il mio indirizzo è ...** [il 'mio indi'rittso e ...]
Your destination?	**La sua destinazione?** [la 'sua destina'tsjone?]
Excuse me, ...	**Mi scusi, ...** [mi 'skuzi, ...]
Are you available?	**E' libero?** [e 'libero?]
How much is it to get to ...?	**Quanto costa andare a ...?** [kwanto 'kosta an'dare a ...?]
Do you know where it is?	**Sapete dove si trova?** [sa'pete 'dove si 'trova?]

Airport, please.	**All'aeroporto, per favore.** [all aero'porto, per fa'vore]
Stop here, please.	**Si fermi qui, per favore.** [si 'fermi kwi, per fa'vore]
It's not here.	**Non è qui.** [non e kwi]
This is the wrong address.	**È l'indirizzo sbagliato.** [e lindi'rittso zbaʎ'ʎato]
Turn left.	**Giri a sinistra.** [dʒiri a si'nistra]
Turn right.	**Giri a destra.** [dʒiri a 'destra]

How much do I owe you?	**Quanto le devo?** [kwanto le 'devo?]
I'd like a receipt, please.	**Potrei avere una ricevuta, per favore.** [po'trej a'vere 'una ritʃe'vuta, per fa'vore]
Keep the change.	**Tenga il resto.** [tenga il 'resto]

Would you please wait for me?	**Può aspettarmi, per favore?** [pu'o aspe'tarmi, per fa'vore?]
five minutes	**cinque minuti** [tʃinkwe mi'nuti]
ten minutes	**dieci minuti** ['djetʃi mi'nuti]
fifteen minutes	**quindici minuti** [kwinditʃi mi'nuti]
twenty minutes	**venti minuti** [venti mi'nuti]
half an hour	**mezzora** [med'dzora]

Hotel

Hello.	**Salve.** [salve]
My name is …	**Mi chiamo …** [mi 'kjamo …]
I have a reservation.	**Ho prenotato una camera.** [o preno'tato 'una 'kamera]
I need …	**Ho bisogno di …** [o bi'zoɲo di …]
a single room	**una camera singola** [una 'kamera 'singola]
a double room	**una camera doppia** [una 'kamera 'doppia]
How much is that?	**Quanto costa questo?** [kwanto 'kosta 'kwesto?]
That's a bit expensive.	**È un po' caro.** [e un 'po 'karo]
Do you have anything else?	**Avete qualcos'altro?** [a'vete kwal'koz 'altro?]
I'll take it.	**La prendo.** [la 'prendo]
I'll pay in cash.	**Pago in contanti.** [pago in kon'tanti]
I've got a problem.	**Ho un problema.** [o un pro'blema]
My … is broken.	**Il mio … è rotto /La mia … è rotta/** [il 'mio … e 'rotto /la 'mia … e 'rotta/]
My … is out of order.	**Il mio /La mia/ … è fuori servizio.** [il 'mio /la 'mia/ … e fu'ori ser'vitsio]
TV	**televisore** [televi'zore]
air conditioner	**condizionatore** [konditsiona'tore]
tap	**rubinetto** [rubi'netto]
shower	**doccia** [dotʃa]
sink	**lavandino** [lavan'dino]
safe	**cassa forte** [kassa 'forte]

door lock	**serratura** [serra'tura]
electrical outlet	**presa elettrica** [preza e'lettrika]
hairdryer	**asciugacapelli** [aʃuga·ka'pelli]

I don't have …	**Non ho …** [non o …]
water	**l'acqua** [lakwa]
light	**la luce** [la 'lutʃe]
electricity	**l'elettricità** [leletritʃi'ta]

Can you give me …?	**Può darmi …?** [pu'o 'darmi …?]
a towel	**un asciugamano** [un aʃuga'mano]
a blanket	**una coperta** [una ko'perta]
slippers	**delle pantofole** [delle pan'tofole]
a robe	**un accappatoio** [un akkappa'tojo]
shampoo	**dello shampoo** [dello 'ʃampo]
soap	**del sapone** [del sa'pone]

I'd like to change rooms.	**Vorrei cambiare la camera.** [vor'rej kam'bjare la 'kamera]
I can't find my key.	**Non trovo la chiave.** [non 'trovo la 'kjave]
Could you open my room, please?	**Potrebbe aprire la mia camera, per favore?** [po'trebbe a'prire la mia 'kamera, per fa'vore?]
Who's there?	**Chi è?** [ki 'e?]
Come in!	**Avanti!** [a'vanti!]
Just a minute!	**Un attimo!** [un 'attimo!]

Not right now, please.	**Non adesso, per favore.** [non a'desso, per fa'vore]
Come to my room, please.	**Può venire nella mia camera, per favore.** [pu'o ve'nire 'nella 'mia 'kamera, per fa'vore]

I'd like to order food service.	**Vorrei ordinare qualcosa da mangiare.** [vor'rej ordi'nare kwal'koza da man'dʒare]
My room number is ...	**Il mio numero di camera è ...** [il 'mio 'numero di 'kamera e ...]

I'm leaving ...	**Parto ...** [parto ...]
We're leaving ...	**Partiamo ...** [par'tjamo ...]
right now	**adesso** [a'desso]
this afternoon	**questo pomeriggio** [kwesto pome'ridʒo]
tonight	**stasera** [sta'sera]
tomorrow	**domani** [do'mani]
tomorrow morning	**domani mattina** [do'mani mat'tina]
tomorrow evening	**domani sera** [do'mani 'sera]
the day after tomorrow	**dopodomani** [dopodo'mani]

I'd like to pay.	**Vorrei pagare.** [vor'rej sal'dare il 'konto]
Everything was wonderful.	**È stato tutto magnifico.** [e 'stato 'tutto ma'ɲifiko]
Where can I get a taxi?	**Dove posso prendere un taxi?** [dove 'posso 'prendere un 'taksi?]
Would you call a taxi for me, please?	**Potrebbe chiamarmi un taxi, per favore?** [po'trebbe kja'marmi un 'taksi, per fa'vore?]

Restaurant

Can I look at the menu, please?

Posso vedere il menù, per favore?
[posso ve'dere il me'nu, per fa'vore?]

Table for one.

Un tavolo per una persona.
[un 'tavolo per 'uno per'sona]

There are two (three, four) of us.

Siamo in due (tre, quattro).
[sjamo in 'due (tre, 'kwattro)]

Smoking

Fumatori
[fuma'tori]

No smoking

Non fumatori
[non fuma'tori]

Excuse me! (addressing a waiter)

Mi scusi!
[mi 'skuzi!]

menu

il menù
[il me'nu]

wine list

la lista dei vini
[la 'lista 'dei 'vini]

The menu, please.

Posso avere il menù, per favore.
[posso a'vere il me'nu, per fa'vore]

Are you ready to order?

È pronto per ordinare?
[e 'pronto per ordi'nare?]

What will you have?

Cosa gradisce?
[koza gra'diʃe?]

I'll have ...

Prendo ...
[prendo ...]

I'm a vegetarian.

Sono vegetariano /vegetariana/.
[sono vedʒeta'rjano /vedʒeta'rjana/]

meat

carne
[karne]

fish

pesce
[peʃe]

vegetables

verdure
[ver'dure]

Do you have vegetarian dishes?

Avete dei piatti vegetariani?
[a'vete 'dei 'pjatti vedʒeta'rjani?]

I don't eat pork.

Non mangio carne di maiale.
[non 'mandʒo 'karne di ma'jale]

Band-Aid

Lui /lei/ non mangia la carne.
[lui /'lei/ non 'mandʒa la 'karne]

I am allergic to ...

Sono allergico a ...
[sono al'lerdʒiko a ...]

Would you please bring me ...

Potrebbe portarmi ...
[po'trebbe por'tarmi ...]

salt | pepper | sugar

del sale | del pepe | dello zucchero
[del 'sale | del 'pepe | 'dello 'tsukkero]

coffee | tea | dessert

un caffè | un tè | un dolce
[un ka'fe | un te | un 'doltʃe]

water | sparkling | plain

dell'acqua | frizzante | naturale
[dell 'akwa | frid'dzante | natu'rale]

a spoon | fork | knife

un cucchiaio | una forchetta | un coltello
[un kuk'kjajo | una for'ketta | un kol'tello]

a plate | napkin

un piatto | un tovagliolo
[un 'pjatto | un tovaʎ'ʎolo]

Enjoy your meal!

Buon appetito!
[bu'on appe'tito!]

One more, please.

Un altro, per favore.
[un 'altro, per fa'vore]

It was very delicious.

È stato squisito.
[e 'stato skwi'zito]

check | change | tip

il conto | il resto | la mancia
[il 'konto | il 'resto | la 'mantʃa]

Check, please.
(Could I have the check, please?)

Il conto, per favore.
[il 'konto, per fa'vore]

Can I pay by credit card?

Posso pagare con la carta di credito?
[posso pa'gare kon la 'karta di 'kredito?]

I'm sorry, there's a mistake here.

Mi scusi, c'è un errore.
[mi 'skuzi, tʃe un er'rore]

Shopping

Can I help you?	**Posso aiutarla?** [posso aju'tarla?]
Do you have ...?	**Avete ...?** [a'vete ...?]
I'm looking for ...	**Sto cercando ...** [sto tʃer'kando ...]
I need ...	**Ho bisogno di ...** [o bi'zoɲo di ...]

I'm just looking.	**Sto guardando.** [sto gwar'dando]
We're just looking.	**Stiamo guardando.** [stjamo gwar'dando]
I'll come back later.	**Ripasserò più tardi.** [ripasse'ro pju 'tardi]
We'll come back later.	**Ripasseremo più tardi.** [ripasse'remo pju 'tardi]
discounts	sale	**sconti	saldi** [skonti	'saldi]

Would you please show me ...	**Per favore, mi può far vedere ...?** [per fa'vore, mi pu'o far ve'dere ...?]
Would you please give me ...	**Per favore, potrebbe darmi ...** [per fa'vore, po'trebbe 'darmi ...]
Can I try it on?	**Posso provarlo?** [posso pro'varlo?]
Excuse me, where's the fitting room?	**Mi scusi, dov'è il camerino?** [mi 'skuzi, dov'e il kame'rino?]
Which color would you like?	**Che colore desidera?** [ke ko'lore de'zidera?]
size	length	**taglia	lunghezza** [taʎʎa	lun'gettsa]
How does it fit?	**Come le sta?** [kome le sta?]

How much is it?	**Quanto costa questo?** [kwanto 'kosta 'kwesto?]
That's too expensive.	**È troppo caro.** [e 'troppo 'karo]
I'll take it.	**Lo prendo.** [lo 'prendo]
Excuse me, where do I pay?	**Mi scusi, dov'è la cassa?** [mi 'skuzi, dov'e la 'kassa?]

Will you pay in cash or credit card?	**Paga in contanti o con carta di credito?** [paga in kon'tanti o kon 'karta di 'kredito?]
In cash | with credit card	**In contanti | con carta di credito** [in kon'tanti | kon 'karta di 'kredito]

Do you want the receipt?	**Vuole lo scontrino?** [vu'ole lo skon'trino?]
Yes, please.	**Si, grazie.** [si, 'gratsie]
No, it's OK.	**No, va bene così.** [no, va 'bene ko'zi]
Thank you. Have a nice day!	**Grazie. Buona giornata!** [gratsie. bu'ona dʒor'nata!]

In town

Excuse me, ...	**Mi scusi, per favore ...** [mi 'skuzi, per fa'vore ...]
I'm looking for ...	**Sto cercando ...** [sto tʃer'kando ...]
the subway	**la metropolitana** [la metropoli'tana]
my hotel	**il mio albergo** [il 'mio al'bergo]
the movie theater	**il cinema** [il 'tʃinema]
a taxi stand	**il posteggio taxi** [il po'stedʒo 'taksi]
an ATM	**un bancomat** [un 'bankomat]
a foreign exchange office	**un ufficio dei cambi** [un uf'fitʃio 'dei 'kambi]
an internet café	**un internet café** [un inter'net ka'fe]
... street	**via ...** [via ...]
this place	**questo posto** [kwesto 'posto]
Do you know where ... is?	**Sa dove si trova ...?** [sa 'dove si 'trova ...?]
Which street is this?	**Come si chiama questa via?** [kome si 'kjama 'kwesta 'via?]
Show me where we are right now.	**Può mostrarmi dove ci troviamo?** [pu'o mo'strarmi 'dove tʃi tro'vjamo]
Can I get there on foot?	**Posso andarci a piedi?** [posso an'dartʃi a 'pjedi?]
Do you have a map of the city?	**Avete la piantina della città?** [a'vete la pjan'tina 'della tʃitta?]
How much is a ticket to get in?	**Quanto costa un biglietto?** [kwanto 'kosta un biʎ'ʎetto?]
Can I take pictures here?	**Si può fotografare?** [si pu'o fotogra'fare?]
Are you open?	**E' aperto?** [e a'perto?]

When do you open?

Quando aprite?
[kwando a'prite?]

When do you close?

Quando chiudete?
[kwando kju'dete?]

Money

money	**Soldi** [soldi]
cash	**contanti** [kon'tanti]
paper money	**banconote** [banko'note]
loose change	**monete** [mo'nete]
check | change | tip	**conto | resto | mancia** [konto | 'resto | 'mantʃa]
credit card	**carta di credito** [karta di 'kredito]
wallet	**portafoglio** [porta·'foʎʎo]
to buy	**comprare** [kom'prare]
to pay	**pagare** [pa'gare]
fine	**multa** [multa]
free	**gratuito** [gratu'ito]
Where can I buy ...?	**Dove posso comprare ...?** [dove 'posso kom'prare ...?]
Is the bank open now?	**La banca è aperta adesso?** [la 'banka e a'perta a'desso?]
When does it open?	**Quando apre?** [kwando 'apre?]
When does it close?	**Quando chiude?** [kwando 'kjude?]
How much?	**Quanto costa?** [kwanto 'kosta?]
How much is this?	**Quanto costa questo?** [kwanto 'kosta 'kwesto?]
That's too expensive.	**È troppo caro.** [e 'troppo 'karo]
Excuse me, where do I pay?	**Scusi, dov'è la cassa?** [skuzi, dov'e la 'kassa?]
Check, please.	**Il conto, per favore.** [il 'konto, per fa'vore]

Can I pay by credit card?

Posso pagare con la carta di credito?
[posso pa'gare kon la 'karta di 'kredito?]

Is there an ATM here?

C'è un bancomat?
[tʃe un 'bankomat?]

I'm looking for an ATM.

Sto cercando un bancomat.
[sto tʃer'kando un 'bankomat]

I'm looking for a foreign exchange office.

Sto cercando un ufficio dei cambi.
[sto tʃer'kando un uf'fitʃio dei 'kambi]

I'd like to change ...

Vorrei cambiare ...
[vor'rej kam'bjare ...]

What is the exchange rate?

Quanto è il tasso di cambio?
[kwanto e il 'tasso di 'kambio]

Do you need my passport?

Ha bisogno del mio passaporto?
[a bi'zoɲo del 'mio passa'porto?]

Time

What time is it?	**Che ore sono?** [ke 'ore 'sono?]
When?	**Quando?** [kwando?]
At what time?	**A che ora?** [a ke 'ora?]
now | later | after …	**adesso | più tardi | dopo …** [a'desso | pju 'tardi | 'dopo …]

one o'clock	**l'una** [luna]
one fifteen	**l'una e un quarto** [luna e un 'kwarto]
one thirty	**l'una e trenta** [luna e 'trenta]
one forty-five	**l'una e quarantacinque** [luna e kwa'ranta 'tʃinkwe]

one | two | three	**uno | due | tre** [uno | 'due | tre]
four | five | six	**quattro | cinque | sei** [kwattro | 'tʃinkwe | sej]
seven | eight | nine	**sette | otto | nove** [sette | 'otto | 'nove]
ten | eleven | twelve	**dieci | undici | dodici** [djetʃi | 'unditʃi | 'doditʃi]

in …	**fra …** [fra …]
five minutes	**cinque minuti** [tʃinkwe mi'nuti]
ten minutes	**dieci minuti** ['djetʃi mi'nuti]
fifteen minutes	**quindici minuti** [kwinditʃi mi'nuti]
twenty minutes	**venti minuti** [venti mi'nuti]
half an hour	**mezzora** [med'dzora]
an hour	**un'ora** [un 'ora]

in the morning	**la mattina** [la mat'tina]
early in the morning	**la mattina presto** [la mat'tina 'presto]
this morning	**questa mattina** [kwesta mat'tina]
tomorrow morning	**domani mattina** [do'mani mat'tina]
in the middle of the day	**all'ora di pranzo** [all 'ora di 'prantso]
in the afternoon	**nel pomeriggio** [nel pome'ridʒo]
in the evening	**la sera** [la 'sera]
tonight	**stasera** [sta'sera]
at night	**la notte** [la 'notte]
yesterday	**ieri** ['jeri]
today	**oggi** [odʒi]
tomorrow	**domani** [do'mani]
the day after tomorrow	**dopodomani** [dopodo'mani]
What day is it today?	**Che giorno è oggi?** [ke 'dʒorno e 'odʒi?]
It's ...	**Oggi è ...** [odʒi e ...?]
Monday	**lunedì** [lune'di]
Tuesday	**martedì** [marte'di]
Wednesday	**mercoledì** [merkole'di]
Thursday	**giovedì** [dʒove'di]
Friday	**venerdì** [vener'di]
Saturday	**sabato** [sabato]
Sunday	**domenica** [do'menika]

Greetings. Introductions

Hello.	**Salve.** [salve]
Pleased to meet you.	**Lieto di conoscerla.** [leto di ko'noʃerla]
Me too.	**Il piacere è mio.** [il pja'tʃere e 'mio]
I'd like you to meet ...	**Vi presento ...** [vi pre'zento ...]
Nice to meet you.	**Molto piacere.** [molto pja'tʃere]
How are you?	**Come sta?** [kome sta?]
My name is ...	**Mi chiamo ...** [mi 'kjamo ...]
His name is ...	**Si chiama ...** [si 'kjama ...]
Her name is ...	**Si chiama ...** [si 'kjama ...]
What's your name?	**Come si chiama?** [kome si 'kjama?]
What's his name?	**Come si chiama lui?** [kome si 'kjama 'lui?]
What's her name?	**Come si chiama lei?** [kome si 'kjama 'lei?]
What's your last name?	**Qual'è il suo cognome?** [kwal e 'suo ko'ɲome?]
You can call me ...	**Può chiamarmi ...** [pu'o kja'marmi ...]
Where are you from?	**Da dove viene?** [da 'dove 'vjene?]
I'm from ...	**Vengo da ...** [vengo da ...]
What do you do for a living?	**Che lavoro fa?** [ke la'voro 'fa?]
Who is this?	**Chi è?** [ki 'e?]
Who is he?	**Chi è lui?** [ki e 'lui?]
Who is she?	**Chi è lei?** [ki e 'lei?]
Who are they?	**Chi sono loro?** [ki 'sono 'loro?]

This is ...	**Questo /Questa/ è ...**
	[kwesto /'kwesta/ e ...]
my friend (masc.)	**il mio amico**
	[il 'mio a'miko]
my friend (fem.)	**la mia amica**
	[la 'mia a'mika]
my husband	**mio marito**
	[mio ma'rito]
my wife	**mia moglie**
	[mia 'moʎʎe]

my father	**mio padre**
	[mio 'padre]
my mother	**mia madre**
	[mia 'madre]
my brother	**mio fratello**
	[mio fra'tello]
my sister	**mia sorella**
	[mia so'rella]
my son	**mio figlio**
	[mio 'fiʎʎo]
my daughter	**mia figlia**
	[mia 'fiʎʎa]

This is our son.	**Questo è nostro figlio.**
	[kwesto e 'nostro 'fiʎʎo]
This is our daughter.	**Questa è nostra figlia.**
	[kwesta e 'nostra 'fiʎʎa]
These are my children.	**Questi sono i miei figli.**
	[kwesti 'sono i 'mjei 'fiʎʎi]
These are our children.	**Questi sono i nostri figli.**
	[kwesti 'sono i 'nostri 'fiʎʎi]

Farewells

Good bye!	**Arrivederci!** [arrive'dertʃi!]
Bye! (inform.)	**Ciao!** [tʃao!]
See you tomorrow.	**A domani.** [a do'mani]
See you soon.	**A presto.** [a 'presto]
See you at seven.	**Ci vediamo alle sette.** [tʃi ve'djamo 'alle 'sette]

Have fun!	**Divertitevi!** [diverti'tevi!]
Talk to you later.	**Ci sentiamo più tardi.** [tʃi sen'tjamo 'pju 'tardi]
Have a nice weekend.	**Buon fine settimana.** [bu'on 'fine setti'mana]
Good night.	**Buona notte** [bu'ona 'notte]

It's time for me to go.	**Adesso devo andare.** [a'desso 'devo an'dare]
I have to go.	**Devo andare.** [devo an'dare]
I will be right back.	**Torno subito.** [torno 'subito]

It's late.	**È tardi.** [e 'tardi]
I have to get up early.	**Domani devo alzarmi presto.** [do'mani 'devo al'tsarmi 'presto]
I'm leaving tomorrow.	**Parto domani.** [parto do'mani]
We're leaving tomorrow.	**Partiamo domani.** [par'tjamo do'mani]

Have a nice trip!	**Buon viaggio!** [bu'on 'vjadʒo!]
It was nice meeting you.	**È stato un piacere conoscerla.** [e 'stato un pja'tʃere di ko'noʃerla]
It was nice talking to you.	**È stato un piacere parlare con lei.** [e 'stato un pja'tʃere par'lare kon lej]
Thanks for everything.	**Grazie di tutto.** [gratsie di 'tutto]

I had a very good time.

Mi sono divertito.
[mi 'sono diver'tito]

We had a very good time.

Ci siamo divertiti.
[ʧi 'sjamo di'vertiti]

It was really great.

È stato straordinario.
[e 'stato straordi'nario]

I'm going to miss you.

Mi mancherà.
[mi maŋke'ra]

We're going to miss you.

Ci mancherà.
[ʧi maŋke'ra]

Good luck!

Buona fortuna!
[bu'ona for'tuna!]

Say hi to ...

Mi saluti ...
[mi sa'luti ...]

Foreign language

I don't understand.	**Non capisco.** [non ka'pisko]
Write it down, please.	**Lo può scrivere, per favore?** [lo pu'o 'skrivere, per fa'vore]
Do you speak ...?	**Parla ...?** [parla ...?]

I speak a little bit of ...	**Parlo un po' ...** [parlo un po ...]
English	**inglese** [in'gleze]
Turkish	**turco** [turko]
Arabic	**arabo** [arabo]
French	**francese** [fran'ʧeze]

German	**tedesco** [te'desko]
Italian	**italiano** [ita'ljano]
Spanish	**spagnolo** [spa'ɲolo]
Portuguese	**portoghese** [porto'geze]
Chinese	**cinese** [ʧi'neze]
Japanese	**giapponese** [dʒappo'neze]

Can you repeat that, please.	**Può ripetere, per favore.** [pu'o ri'petere, per fa'vore]
I understand.	**Capisco.** [ka'pisko]
I don't understand.	**Non capisco.** [non ka'pisko]
Please speak more slowly.	**Può parlare più piano, per favore.** [pu'o par'lare pju 'pjano, per fa'vore]

Is that correct? (Am I saying it right?)	**È corretto?** [e kor'retto?]
What is this? (What does this mean?)	**Cos'è questo?** [koz e 'kwesto?]

Apologies

Excuse me, please.

Mi scusi, per favore.
[mi 'skuzi, per fa'vore]

I'm sorry.

Mi dispiace.
[mi dis'pjatʃe]

I'm really sorry.

Mi dispiace molto.
[mi dis'pjatʃe 'molto]

Sorry, it's my fault.

Mi dispiace, è colpa mia.
[mi dis'pjatʃe, e 'kolpa 'mia]

My mistake.

È stato un mio errore.
[e 'stato un 'mio er'rore]

May I ...?

Posso ...?
[posso ...?]

Do you mind if I ...?

Le dispiace se ...?
[le dis'pjatʃe se ...?]

It's OK.

Non fa niente.
[non fa 'njente]

It's all right.

Tutto bene.
[tutto 'bene]

Don't worry about it.

Non si preoccupi.
[non si pre'okkupi]

Agreement

Yes.	**Sì.** [si]
Yes, sure.	**Sì, certo.** [si, 'tʃerto]
OK (Good!)	**Bene.** [bene]
Very well.	**Molto bene.** [molto 'bene]
Certainly!	**Certamente!** [tʃerta'mente!]
I agree.	**Sono d'accordo.** [sono dak'kordo]
That's correct.	**Esatto.** [e'satto]
That's right.	**Giusto.** [dʒusto]
You're right.	**Ha ragione.** [a ra'dʒone]
I don't mind.	**È lo stesso.** [e lo 'stesso]
Absolutely right.	**È assolutamente corretto.** [e assoluta'mente kor'retto]
It's possible.	**È possibile.** [e pos'sibile]
That's a good idea.	**È una buona idea.** [e 'una bu'ona i'dea]
I can't say no.	**Non posso dire di no.** [non 'posso 'dire di no]
I'd be happy to.	**Ne sarei lieto.** [ne sa'rei 'leto]
With pleasure.	**Con piacere.** [kon pja'tʃere]

Refusal. Expressing doubt

No.	**No.** [no]
Certainly not.	**Sicuramente no.** [sikura'mente no]
I don't agree.	**Non sono d'accordo.** [non 'sono dak'kordo]
I don't think so.	**Non penso.** [non 'penso]
It's not true.	**Non è vero.** [non e 'vero]
You are wrong.	**Si sbaglia.** [si 'zbaʎʎa]
I think you are wrong.	**Penso che lei si stia sbagliando.** [penso ke 'lei si stia zbaʎ'ʎando]
I'm not sure.	**Non sono sicuro.** [non 'sono si'kuro]
It's impossible.	**È impossibile.** [e impos'sibile]
Nothing of the kind (sort)!	**Assolutamente no!** [assoluta'mente no!]
The exact opposite.	**Esattamente il contrario!** [ezatta'mente al kon'trario!]
I'm against it.	**Sono contro.** [sono 'kontro]
I don't care.	**Non m'interessa.** [non minte'ressa]
I have no idea.	**Non ne ho idea.** [non ne o i'dea]
I doubt it.	**Dubito che sia così.** [dubito ke 'sia ko'zi]
Sorry, I can't.	**Mi dispiace, non posso.** [mi dis'pjatʃe, non 'posso]
Sorry, I don't want to.	**Mi dispiace, non voglio.** [mi dis'pjatʃe, non 'voʎʎo]
Thank you, but I don't need this.	**Non ne ho bisogno, grazie.** [non ne o bi'zoɲo, 'gratsie]
It's getting late.	**È già tardi.** [e dʒa 'tardi]

I have to get up early.	**Devo alzarmi presto.** [devo alts'armi 'presto]
I don't feel well.	**Non mi sento bene.** [non mi 'sento 'bene]

Expressing gratitude

Thank you.	**Grazie.** [gratsie]
Thank you very much.	**Grazie mille.** [gratsie 'mille]
I really appreciate it.	**Le sono riconoscente.** [le 'sono rikono'ʃente]
I'm really grateful to you.	**Le sono davvero grato.** [le 'sono dav'vero 'grato]
We are really grateful to you.	**Le siamo davvero grati.** [le 'sjamo dav'vero 'grati]
Thank you for your time.	**Grazie per la sua disponibilità.** [gratsie per la 'sua disponibili'ta]
Thanks for everything.	**Grazie di tutto.** [gratsie di 'tutto]
Thank you for ...	**Grazie per ...** [gratsie per ...]
your help	**il suo aiuto** [il 'suo a'juto]
a nice time	**il bellissimo tempo** [il bel'lissimo 'tempo]
a wonderful meal	**il delizioso pranzo** [il deli'tsjozo 'prantso]
a pleasant evening	**la bella serata** [la 'bella se'rata]
a wonderful day	**la bella giornata** [la 'bella dʒor'nata]
an amazing journey	**la splendida gita** [la 'splendida 'dʒita]
Don't mention it.	**Non c'è di che.** [non ʧe di 'ke]
You are welcome.	**Prego.** [prego]
Any time.	**Con piacere.** [kon pja'ʧere]
My pleasure.	**È stato un piacere.** [e 'stato un pja'ʧere]
Forget it.	**Non ci pensi neanche.** [non ʧi 'pensi ne'aŋke]
Don't worry about it.	**Non si preoccupi.** [non si pre'okkupi]

Congratulations. Best wishes

Congratulations!	**Congratulazioni!** [kongratula'tsjoni!]
Happy birthday!	**Buon compleanno!** [bu'on komple'anno!]
Merry Christmas!	**Buon Natale!** [bu'on na'tale!]
Happy New Year!	**Felice Anno Nuovo!** [fe'litʃe 'anno nu'ovo!]
Happy Easter!	**Buona Pasqua!** [bu'ona 'paskwa!]
Happy Hanukkah!	**Felice Hanukkah!** [fe'litʃe anu'ka!]
I'd like to propose a toast.	**Vorrei fare un brindisi.** [vor'rej 'fare un 'brindizi]
Cheers!	**Salute!** [sa'lute!]
Let's drink to …!	**Beviamo a …!** [be'vjamo a …!]
To our success!	**Al nostro successo!** [al 'nostro su'tʃesso!]
To your success!	**Al suo successo!** [al 'suo su'tʃesso!]
Good luck!	**Buona fortuna!** [bu'ona for'tuna!]
Have a nice day!	**Buona giornata!** [bu'ona dʒor'nata!]
Have a good holiday!	**Buone vacanze!** [bu'one va'kantse!]
Have a safe journey!	**Buon viaggio!** [bu'on 'vjadʒo!]
I hope you get better soon!	**Spero guarisca presto!** [spero gwa'riska 'presto!]

Socializing

Why are you sad?	**Perché è triste?** [per'ke e 'triste?]
Smile! Cheer up!	**Sorrida!** [sor'rida!]
Are you free tonight?	**È libero stasera?** [e 'libero sta'sera?]

May I offer you a drink?	**Posso offrirle qualcosa da bere?** [posso of'frirle kwal'koza da 'bere?]
Would you like to dance?	**Vuole ballare?** [vu'ole bal'lare?]
Let's go to the movies.	**Andiamo al cinema.** [an'djamo al 'tʃinema]

May I invite you to ...?	**Posso invitarla ...?** [posso invi'tarla ...?]
a restaurant	**al ristorante** [al risto'rante]
the movies	**al cinema** [al 'tʃinema]
the theater	**a teatro** [a te'atro]
go for a walk	**a fare una passeggiata** [per 'fare 'una passe'dʒata]

At what time?	**A che ora?** [a ke 'ora?]
tonight	**stasera** [sta'sera]
at six	**alle sei** [alle 'sei]
at seven	**alle sette** [alle 'sette]
at eight	**alle otto** [alle 'otto]
at nine	**alle nove** [alle 'nove]

Do you like it here?	**Le piace qui?** [le 'pjatʃe kwi?]
Are you here with someone?	**È qui con qualcuno?** [e kw'i kon kwal'kuno?]
I'm with my friend.	**Sono con un amico /una amica/.** [sono kon un a'miko /'una a'mika/]

I'm with my friends.	**Sono con i miei amici.** [sono kon i mjei a'mitʃi]
No, I'm alone.	**No, sono da solo /sola/.** [no, 'sono da 'solo /'sola/]

Do you have a boyfriend?	**Hai il ragazzo?** [ai il ra'gattso?]
I have a boyfriend.	**Ho il ragazzo.** [o il ra'gattso]
Do you have a girlfriend?	**Hai la ragazza?** [ai il ra'gattsa?]
I have a girlfriend.	**Ho la ragazza.** [o la ra'gattsa]

Can I see you again?	**Posso rivederti?** [posso rive'derti?]
Can I call you?	**Posso chiamarti?** [posso kja'marti?]
Call me. (Give me a call.)	**Chiamami.** ['kjamami]
What's your number?	**Qual'è il tuo numero?** [kwal e il 'tuo 'numero?]
I miss you.	**Mi manchi.** [mi 'maŋki]

You have a beautiful name.	**Ha un bel nome.** [a un bel 'nome]
I love you.	**Ti amo.** [ti 'amo]
Will you marry me?	**Mi vuoi sposare?** [mi vu'oj spo'zare?]
You're kidding!	**Sta scherzando!** [sta sker'tsando!]
I'm just kidding.	**Sto scherzando.** [sto sker'tsando]

Are you serious?	**Lo dice sul serio?** [lo 'ditʃe sul 'serio?]
I'm serious.	**Sono serio /seria/.** [sono 'serio /'seria/]
Really?!	**Davvero?!** [dav'vero?!]
It's unbelievable!	**È incredibile!** [e inkre'dibile]
I don't believe you.	**Non le credo.** [non le 'kredo]
I can't.	**Non posso.** [non 'posso]
I don't know.	**No so.** [non so]
I don't understand you.	**Non la capisco.** [non la ka'pisko]

Please go away.

Per favore, vada via.
[per fa'vore, 'vada 'via]

Leave me alone!

Mi lasci in pace!
[mi 'laʃi in 'patʃe!]

I can't stand him.

Non lo sopporto.
[non lo sop'porto]

You are disgusting!

Lei è disgustoso!
[lei e dizgu'stozo!]

I'll call the police!

Chiamo la polizia!
[kjamo la poli'tsia!]

Sharing impressions. Emotions

I like it.	**Mi piace.** [mi 'pjatʃe]
Very nice.	**Molto carino.** [molto ka'rino]
That's great!	**È formidabile!** [e formi'dabile!]
It's not bad.	**Non è male.** [non e 'male]

I don't like it.	**Non mi piace.** [non mi 'pjatʃe]
It's not good.	**Questo non è buono.** [kwesto non e bu'ono]
It's bad.	**È cattivo.** [e kat'tivo]
It's very bad.	**È molto cattivo.** [e 'molto kat'tivo]
It's disgusting.	**È disgustoso.** [e dizgu'stozo]

I'm happy.	**Sono felice.** [sono fe'litʃe]
I'm content.	**Sono contento /contenta/.** [sono kon'tento /kon'tenta/]
I'm in love.	**Sono innamorato /innamorata/.** [sono innamo'rato /innamo'rata/]
I'm calm.	**Sono calmo /calma/.** [sono 'kalmo /'kalma/]
I'm bored.	**Sono annoiato /annoiata/.** [sono anno'jato /anno'jata/]

I'm tired.	**Sono stanco /stanca/.** [sono 'stanko /'stanka/]
I'm sad.	**Sono triste.** [sono 'triste]
I'm frightened.	**Sono spaventato /spaventata/.** [sono spaven'tato /spaven'tata/]

I'm angry.	**Sono arrabbiato /arrabbiata/.** [sono arrab'bjato /arrab'bjata/]
I'm worried.	**Sono preoccupato /preoccupata/.** [sono preokku'pato /preokku'pata/]
I'm nervous.	**Sono nervoso /nervosa/.** [sono ner'vozo /ner'voza/]

I'm jealous. (envious)

Sono geloso /gelosa/.
[sono ʤe'lozo /ʤe'loza/]

I'm surprised.

Sono sorpreso /sorpresa/.
[sono sor'prezo /sor'preza/]

I'm perplexed.

Sono perplesso /perplessa/.
[sono per'plesso /per'plessa/]

Problems. Accidents

I've got a problem.	**Ho un problema.** [o un pro'blema]
We've got a problem.	**Abbiamo un problema.** [ab'bjamo un pro'blema]
I'm lost.	**Sono perso /persa/.** [sono' perso /'persa/]
I missed the last bus (train).	**Ho perso l'ultimo autobus (treno).** [o 'perso 'lultimo 'autobus ('treno)]
I don't have any money left.	**Non ho più soldi.** [non o pju 'soldi]

I've lost my ...	**Ho perso ...** [o 'perso ...]
Someone stole my ...	**Mi hanno rubato ...** [mi 'anno ru'bato ...]
passport	**il passaporto** [il passa'porto]
wallet	**il portafoglio** [il porta'foʎʎo]
papers	**i documenti** [i doku'menti]
ticket	**il biglietto** [il biʎ'ʎetto]

money	**i soldi** [i 'soldi]
handbag	**la borsa** [la 'borsa]
camera	**la macchina fotografica** [la 'makkina foto'grafika]
laptop	**il computer portatile** [il kom'pjuter por'tatile]
tablet computer	**il tablet** [il 'tablet]
mobile phone	**il telefono cellulare** [il te'lefono tʃellu'lare]

Help me!	**Aiuto!** [a'juto]
What's happened?	**Che cosa è successo?** [ke 'koza e su'tʃesso?]
fire	**fuoco** [fu'oko]

shooting	**sparatoria** [spara'toria]
murder	**omicidio** [omi'tʃidio]
explosion	**esplosione** [esplo'zjone]
fight	**rissa** ['rissa]

Call the police!	**Chiamate la polizia!** [kja'mate la poli'tsia!]
Please hurry up!	**Per favore, faccia presto!** [per fa'vore, 'fatʃa 'presto!]
I'm looking for the police station.	**Sto cercando la stazione di polizia.** [sto tʃer'kando la sta'tsjone di poli'tsia]
I need to make a call.	**Devo fare una telefonata.** [devo 'fare 'una telefo'nata]
May I use your phone?	**Posso usare il suo telefono?** [posso u'zare il 'suo te'lefono?]

I've been …	**Sono stato /stata/ …** [sono 'stato /'stata/ …]
mugged	**aggredito /aggredita/** [ag'gredito /ag'gredita/]
robbed	**derubato /derubata/** [deru'bato /deru'bata/]
raped	**violentata** [violen'tata]
attacked (beaten up)	**assalito /assalita/** [assa'lito /assa'lita/]

Are you all right?	**Lei sta bene?** [lei sta 'bene?]
Did you see who it was?	**Ha visto chi è stato?** [a 'visto ki e 'stato?]
Would you be able to recognize the person?	**È in grado di riconoscere la persona?** [e in 'grado di riko'noʃere la per'sona?]
Are you sure?	**È sicuro?** [e si'kuro?]

Please calm down.	**Per favore, si calmi.** [per fa'vore, si 'kalmi]
Take it easy!	**Si calmi!** [si 'kalmi!]
Don't worry!	**Non si preoccupi.** [non si pre'okkupi]
Everything will be fine.	**Andrà tutto bene.** [and'ra 'tutto 'bene]
Everything's all right.	**Va tutto bene.** [va 'tutto 'bene]
Come here, please.	**Venga qui, per favore.** [venga kwi, per fa'vore]

I have some questions for you.	**Devo porle qualche domanda.** [devo 'porle 'kwalke do'manda]
Wait a moment, please.	**Aspetti un momento, per favore.** [a'spetti un mo'mento, per fa'vore]
Do you have any I.D.?	**Ha un documento d'identità?** [a un doku'mento didenti'ta?]
Thanks. You can leave now.	**Grazie. Può andare ora.** [gratsie. pu'o an'dare 'ora]
Hands behind your head!	**Mani dietro la testa!** [mani 'djetro la 'testa!]
You're under arrest!	**È in arresto!** [e in ar'resto!]

Health problems

Please help me.	**Mi può aiutare, per favore.** [mi pu'o aju'tare, per fa'vore]
I don't feel well.	**Non mi sento bene.** [non mi 'sento 'bene]
My husband doesn't feel well.	**Mio marito non si sente bene.** [mio ma'rito non si 'sente 'bene]
My son ...	**Mio figlio ...** [mio 'fiʎʎo ...]
My father ...	**Mio padre ...** [mio 'padre ...]

My wife doesn't feel well.	**Mia moglie non si sente bene.** [mia 'moʎʎe non si 'sente 'bene]
My daughter ...	**Mia figlia ...** [mia 'fiʎʎa ...]
My mother ...	**Mia madre ...** [mia 'madre ...]

I've got a ...	**Ho mal di ...** [o mal di ...]
headache	**testa** [testa]
sore throat	**gola** [gola]
stomach ache	**pancia** ['pantʃa]
toothache	**denti** [denti]

I feel dizzy.	**Mi gira la testa.** [mi 'dʒira la 'testa]
He has a fever.	**Ha la febbre.** [a la 'febbre]
She has a fever.	**Ha la febbre.** [a la 'febbre]
I can't breathe.	**Non riesco a respirare.** [non ri'esko a respi'rare]

I'm short of breath.	**Mi manca il respiro.** [mi 'manka il re'spiro]
I am asthmatic.	**Sono asmatico /asmatica/.** [sono az'matiko /az'matika/]
I am diabetic.	**Sono diabetico /diabetica/.** [sono dia'betiko /dia'betika/]

I can't sleep.	**Soffro d'insonnia.** [soffro din'sonnia]
food poisoning	**intossicazione alimentare** [intossikat'tsjone alimen'tare]

It hurts here.	**Fa male qui.** [fa 'male kwi]
Help me!	**Mi aiuti!** [mi a'juti!]
I am here!	**Sono qui!** [sono kwi!]
We are here!	**Siamo qui!** [sjamo kwi!]
Get me out of here!	**Mi tiri fuori di qui!** [mi 'tiri fu'ori di kwi!]
I need a doctor.	**Ho bisogno di un dottore.** [o bi'zoɲo di un dot'tore]
I can't move.	**Non riesco a muovermi.** [non ri'esko a mu'overmi]
I can't move my legs.	**Non riesco a muovere le gambe.** [non ri'esko a mu'overe le 'gambe]

I have a wound.	**Ho una ferita.** [o 'una fe'rita]
Is it serious?	**È grave?** [e 'grave?]
My documents are in my pocket.	**I miei documenti sono in tasca.** [i 'mjei doku'menti 'sono in 'taska]
Calm down!	**Si calmi!** [si 'kalmi!]
May I use your phone?	**Posso usare il suo telefono?** [posso u'zare il 'suo te'lefono?]

Call an ambulance!	**Chiamate l'ambulanza!** [kja'mate lambu'lantsa!]
It's urgent!	**È urgente!** [e ur'dʒente!]
It's an emergency!	**È un'emergenza!** [e un emer'dʒentsa!]
Please hurry up!	**Per favore, faccia presto!** [per fa'vore, 'fatʃa 'presto!]
Would you please call a doctor?	**Per favore, chiamate un medico.** [per fa'vore, kja'mate un 'mediko]
Where is the hospital?	**Dov'è l'ospedale?** [dov'e lospe'dale?]

How are you feeling?	**Come si sente?** [kome si 'sente?]
Are you all right?	**Sta bene?** [sta 'bene?]
What's happened?	**Che cosa è successo?** [ke 'koza e su'tʃesso?]

I feel better now.

Mi sento meglio ora.
[mi 'sento 'meʎʎo 'ora]

It's OK.

Va bene.
[va 'bene]

It's all right.

Va tutto bene.
[va 'tutto 'bene]

At the pharmacy

pharmacy (drugstore)	**farmacia** [farma'tʃija]
24-hour pharmacy	**farmacia di turno** [farma'tʃija di 'turno]
Where is the closest pharmacy?	**Dov'è la farmacia più vicina?** [dov'e la farma'tʃija pju vi'tʃina?]
Is it open now?	**È aperta a quest'ora?** [e a'perta a 'kwest 'ora?]
At what time does it open?	**A che ora apre?** [a ke 'ora 'apre?]
At what time does it close?	**A che ora chiude?** [a ke 'ora 'kjude?]
Is it far?	**È lontana?** [e lon'tana?]
Can I get there on foot?	**Posso andarci a piedi?** [posso an'dartʃi a 'pjedi?]
Can you show me on the map?	**Può mostrarmi sulla piantina?** [pu'o mo'strarmi 'sulla pjan'tina?]
Please give me something for ...	**Per favore, può darmi qualcosa per ...** [per fa'vore, pu'o 'darmi kwal'koza per ...]
a headache	**il mal di testa** [il mal di 'testa]
a cough	**la tosse** [la 'tosse]
a cold	**il raffreddore** [il raffred'dore]
the flu	**l'influenza** [linflu'entsa]
a fever	**la febbre** [la 'febbre]
a stomach ache	**il mal di stomaco** [il mal di 'stomako]
nausea	**la nausea** [la 'nauzea]
diarrhea	**la diarrea** [la diar'rea]
constipation	**la costipazione** [la kostipa'tsjone]
pain in the back	**mal di schiena** [mal di 'skjena]

chest pain

dolore al petto
[do'lore al 'petto]

side stitch

fitte al fianco
[fitte al 'fjanko]

abdominal pain

dolori addominali
[do'lori addomi'nali]

pill

pastiglia
[pa'stiʎʎa]

ointment, cream

pomata
[po'mata]

syrup

sciroppo
[ʃi'roppo]

spray

spray
[spraj]

drops

gocce
[gotʃe]

You need to go to the hospital.

Deve andare in ospedale.
[deve an'dare in ospe'dale]

health insurance

assicurazione sanitaria
[assikura'tsjone sani'taria]

prescription

prescrizione
[preskri'tsjone]

insect repellant

insettifugo
[inset'tifugo]

Band Aid

cerotto
[tʃe'rotto]

The bare minimum

Excuse me, ...	**Mi scusi, ...** [mi 'skuzi, ...]
Hello.	**Buongiorno.** [buon'dʒorno]
Thank you.	**Grazie.** [gratsie]
Good bye.	**Arrivederci.** [arrive'dertʃi]
Yes.	**Sì.** [si]
No.	**No.** [no]
I don't know.	**Non lo so.** [non lo so]
Where? | Where to? | When?	**Dove? | Dove? | Quando?** [dove? | 'dove? | 'kwando?]
I need ...	**Ho bisogno di ...** [o bi'zoɲo di ...]
I want ...	**Voglio ...** [voʎʎo ...]
Do you have ...?	**Avete ...?** [a'vete ...?]
Is there a ... here?	**C'è un /una/ ... qui?** [tʃe un /'una/ ... kwi?]
May I ...?	**Posso ...?** [posso ...?]
..., please (polite request)	**per favore** [per fa'vore]
I'm looking for ...	**Sto cercando ...** [sto tʃer'kando ...]
the restroom	**bagno** [baɲo]
an ATM	**bancomat** [bankomat]
a pharmacy (drugstore)	**farmacia** [farma'tʃija]
a hospital	**ospedale** [ospe'dale]
the police station	**stazione di polizia** [sta'tsjone di poli'tsia]
the subway	**metropolitana** [metropoli'tana]

a taxi	**taxi** ['taksi]
the train station	**stazione** [sta'tsjone]

My name is ...	**Mi chiamo ...** [mi 'kjamo ...]
What's your name?	**Come si chiama?** [kome si 'kjama?]
Could you please help me?	**Mi può aiutare, per favore?** [mi pu'o aju'tare, per fa'vore?]
I've got a problem.	**Ho un problema.** [o un pro'blema]
I don't feel well.	**Mi sento male.** [mi 'sento 'male]
Call an ambulance!	**Chiamate l'ambulanza!** [kja'mate lambu'lantsa!]
May I make a call?	**Posso fare una telefonata?** [posso 'fare 'una telefo'nata?]

I'm sorry.	**Mi dispiace.** [mi dis'pjatʃe]
You're welcome.	**Prego.** [prego]

I, me	**io** [io]
you (inform.)	**tu** [tu]
he	**lui** [lui]
she	**lei** ['lei]
they (masc.)	**loro** [loro]
they (fem.)	**loro** [loro]
we	**noi** [noi]
you (pl)	**voi** [voi]
you (sg, form.)	**Lei** ['lei]

ENTRANCE	**ENTRATA** [en'trata]
EXIT	**USCITA** [u'ʃita]
OUT OF ORDER	**FUORI SERVIZIO** [fu'ori ser'vitsio]
CLOSED	**CHIUSO** [kjuzo]

OPEN	**APERTO** [a'perto]
FOR WOMEN	**DONNE** [donne]
FOR MEN	**UOMINI** [u'omini]

T&P BOOKS

TOPICAL VOCABULARY

This section contains more than 3,000 of the most important words.
The dictionary will provide invaluable assistance while traveling abroad, because frequently individual words are enough for you to be understood.
The dictionary includes a convenient transcription of each foreign word

T&P Books Publishing

VOCABULARY
CONTENTS

T&P Books Publishing

BASIC CONCEPTS

T&P Books Publishing

1. Pronouns

I, me	**io**	['io]
you	**tu**	['tu]
he	**lui**	['luj]
she	**lei**	['lej]
we	**noi**	['noj]
you (to a group)	**voi**	['voi]
they	**loro, essi**	['loro], ['essi]

2. Greetings. Salutations

Hello! (fam.)	**Buongiorno!**	[buon'dʒorno]
Hello! (form.)	**Salve!**	['salve]
Good morning!	**Buongiorno!**	[buon'dʒorno]
Good afternoon!	**Buon pomeriggio!**	[bu'on pome'ridʒo]
Good evening!	**Buonasera!**	[buona'sera]
to say hello	**salutare** (vt)	[salu'tare]
Hi! (hello)	**Ciao! Salve!**	['tʃao], ['salve]
greeting (n)	**saluto** (m)	[sa'luto]
to greet (vt)	**salutare** (vt)	[salu'tare]
How are you?	**Come va?**	['kome 'va]
What's new?	**Che c'è di nuovo?**	[ke tʃe di nu'ovo]
Bye-Bye! Goodbye!	**Arrivederci!**	[arrive'dertʃi]
See you soon!	**A presto!**	[a 'presto]
Farewell!	**Addio!**	[ad'dio]
to say goodbye	**congedarsi** (vr)	[kondʒe'darsi]
So long!	**Ciao!**	['tʃao]
Thank you!	**Grazie!**	['gratsie]
Thank you very much!	**Grazie mille!**	['gratsie 'mille]
You're welcome	**Prego**	['prego]
Don't mention it!	**Non c'è di che!**	[non tʃe di 'ke]
It was nothing	**Di niente**	[di 'njente]
Excuse me! (fam.)	**Scusa!**	['skuza]
Excuse me! (form.)	**Scusi!**	['skuzi]
to excuse (forgive)	**scusare** (vt)	[sku'zare]
to apologize (vi)	**scusarsi** (vr)	[sku'zarsi]
My apologies	**Chiedo scusa**	['kjedo 'skuza]

I'm sorry!	Mi perdoni!	[mi per'doni]
to forgive (vt)	perdonare (vt)	[perdo'nare]
It's okay! (that's all right)	Non fa niente	[non fa 'njente]
please (adv)	per favore	[per fa'vore]

Don't forget!	Non dimentichi!	[non di'mentiki]
Certainly!	Certamente!	[tʃerta'mente]
Of course not!	Certamente no!	[tʃerta'mente no]
Okay! (I agree)	D'accordo!	[dak'kordo]
That's enough!	Basta!	['basta]

3. Questions

Who?	Chi?	[ki]
What?	Che cosa?	[ke 'koza]
Where? (at, in)	Dove?	['dove]
Where (to)?	Dove?	['dove]
From where?	Di dove?, Da dove?	[di 'dove], [da 'dove]
When?	Quando?	['kwando]
Why? (What for?)	Perché?	[per'ke]
Why? (~ are you crying?)	Perché?	[per'ke]

What for?	Per che cosa?	[per ke 'koza]
How? (in what way)	Come?	['kome]
What? (What kind of …?)	Che?	[ke]
Which?	Quale?	['kwale]

To whom?	A chi?	[a 'ki]
About whom?	Di chi?	[di 'ki]
About what?	Di che cosa?	[di ke 'koza]
With whom?	Con chi?	[kon 'ki]

How many?	Quanti?	['kwanti]
How much?	Quanto?	['kwanto]
Whose?	Di chi?	[di 'ki]

4. Prepositions

with (accompanied by)	con	[kon]
without	senza	['sentsa]
to (indicating direction)	a	[a]
about (talking ~ …)	di	[di]
before (in time)	prima di …	['prima di]
in front of …	di fronte a …	[di 'fronte a]

under (beneath, below)	sotto	['sotto]
above (over)	sopra	['sopra]
on (atop)	su	[su]

| from (off, out of) | da, di | [da], [di] |
| of (made from) | di | [di] |

| in (e.g., ~ ten minutes) | fra ... | [fra] |
| over (across the top of) | attraverso | [attra'verso] |

5. Function words. Adverbs. Part 1

Where? (at, in)	Dove?	['dove]
here (adv)	qui	[kwi]
there (adv)	lì	[li]

| somewhere (to be) | da qualche parte | [da 'kwalke 'parte] |
| nowhere (not in any place) | da nessuna parte | [da nes'suna 'parte] |

| by (near, beside) | vicino a ... | [vi'tʃino a] |
| by the window | vicino alla finestra | [vi'tʃino 'alla fi'nestra] |

Where (to)?	Dove?	['dove]
here (e.g., come ~!)	di qui	[di kwi]
there (e.g., to go ~)	ci	[tʃi]
from here (adv)	da qui	[da kwi]
from there (adv)	da lì	[da 'li]

| close (adv) | vicino, accanto | [vi'tʃino], [a'kanto] |
| far (adv) | lontano | [lon'tano] |

near (e.g., ~ Paris)	vicino a ...	[vi'tʃino a]
nearby (adv)	vicino	[vi'tʃino]
not far (adv)	non lontano	[non lon'tano]

left (adj)	sinistro	[si'nistro]
on the left	a sinistra	[a si'nistra]
to the left	a sinistra	[a si'nistra]

right (adj)	destro	['destro]
on the right	a destra	[a 'destra]
to the right	a destra	[a 'destra]

in front (adv)	davanti	[da'vanti]
front (as adj)	anteriore	[ante'rjore]
ahead (the kids ran ~)	avanti	[a'vanti]

behind (adv)	dietro	['djetro]
from behind	da dietro	[da 'djetro]
back (towards the rear)	indietro	[in'djetro]

middle	mezzo (m), centro (m)	['meddzo], ['tʃentro]
in the middle	in mezzo, al centro	[in 'meddzo], [al 'tʃentro]
at the side	di fianco	[di 'fjanko]

everywhere (adv)	**dappertutto**	[dapper'tutto]
around (in all directions)	**attorno**	[at'torno]
from inside	**da dentro**	[da 'dentro]
somewhere (to go)	**da qualche parte**	[da 'kwalke 'parte]
straight (directly)	**dritto**	['dritto]
back (e.g., come ~)	**indietro**	[in'djetro]
from anywhere	**da qualsiasi parte**	[da kwal'siazi 'parte]
from somewhere	**da qualche posto**	[da 'kwalke 'posto]
firstly (adv)	**in primo luogo**	[in 'primo lu'ogo]
secondly (adv)	**in secondo luogo**	[in se'kondo lu'ogo]
thirdly (adv)	**in terzo luogo**	[in 'tertso lu'ogo]
suddenly (adv)	**all'improvviso**	[all improv'vizo]
at first (in the beginning)	**all'inizio**	[all i'nitsio]
for the first time	**per la prima volta**	[per la 'prima 'volta]
long before ...	**molto tempo prima di ...**	['molto 'tempo 'prima di]
anew (over again)	**di nuovo**	[di nu'ovo]
for good (adv)	**per sempre**	[per 'sempre]
never (adv)	**mai**	[maj]
again (adv)	**ancora**	[an'kora]
now (at present)	**adesso**	[a'desso]
often (adv)	**spesso**	['spesso]
then (adv)	**allora**	[al'lora]
urgently (quickly)	**urgentemente**	[urdʒente'mente]
usually (adv)	**di solito**	[di 'solito]
by the way, ...	**a proposito, ...**	[a pro'pozito]
possibly	**è possibile**	[e pos'sibile]
probably (adv)	**probabilmente**	[probabil'mente]
maybe (adv)	**forse**	['forse]
besides ...	**inoltre ...**	[i'noltre]
that's why ...	**ecco perché ...**	['ekko per'ke]
in spite of ...	**nonostante**	[nono'stante]
thanks to ...	**grazie a ...**	['gratsie a]
what (pron.)	**che cosa**	[ke 'koza]
that (conj.)	**che**	[ke]
something	**qualcosa**	[kwal'koza]
anything (something)	**qualcosa**	[kwal'koza]
nothing	**niente**	['njente]
who (pron.)	**chi**	[ki]
someone	**qualcuno**	[kwal'kuno]
somebody	**qualcuno**	[kwal'kuno]
nobody	**nessuno**	[nes'suno]
nowhere (a voyage to ~)	**da nessuna parte**	[da nes'suna 'parte]
nobody's	**di nessuno**	[di nes'suno]

somebody's	di qualcuno	[di kwal'kuno]
so (I'm ~ glad)	così	[ko'zi]
also (as well)	anche	['aŋke]
too (as well)	anche, pure	['aŋke], ['pure]

6. Function words. Adverbs. Part 2

Why?	Perché?	[per'ke]
for some reason	per qualche ragione	[per 'kwalke ra'dʒone]
because ...	perché ...	[per'ke]
for some purpose	per qualche motivo	[per 'kwalke mo'tivo]

and	e	[e]
or	o ...	[o]
but	ma	[ma]
for (e.g., ~ me)	per	[per]

too (~ many people)	troppo	['troppo]
only (exclusively)	solo	['solo]
exactly (adv)	esattamente	[ezatta'mente]
about (more or less)	circa	['tʃirka]

approximately (adv)	approssimativamente	[approsimativa'mente]
approximate (adj)	approssimativo	[approssima'tivo]
almost (adv)	quasi	['kwazi]
the rest	resto (m)	['resto]

each (adj)	ogni	['oɲi]
any (no matter which)	qualsiasi	[kwal'siazi]
many (adj)	molti	['molti]
much (adv)	molto	['molto]
many people	molta gente	['molta 'dʒente]
all (everyone)	tutto, tutti	['tutto], ['tutti]

| in return for ... | in cambio di ... | [in 'kambio di] |
| in exchange (adv) | in cambio | [in 'kambio] |

| by hand (made) | a mano | [a 'mano] |
| hardly (negative opinion) | poco probabile | ['poko pro'babile] |

probably (adv)	probabilmente	[probabil'mente]
on purpose (intentionally)	apposta	[ap'posta]
by accident (adv)	per caso	[per 'kazo]

very (adv)	molto	['molto]
for example (adv)	per esempio	[per e'zempjo]
between	fra	[fra]
among	fra	[fra]
so much (such a lot)	tanto	['tanto]
especially (adv)	soprattutto	[sopra'tutto]

T&P BOOKS

NUMBERS.
MISCELLANEOUS

T&P Books Publishing

0 zero	zero (m)	['dzero]
1 one	uno	['uno]
2 two	due	['due]
3 three	tre	['tre]
4 four	quattro	['kwattro]
5 five	cinque	['tʃinkwe]
6 six	sei	['sej]
7 seven	sette	['sette]
8 eight	otto	['otto]
9 nine	nove	['nove]
10 ten	dieci	['djetʃi]
11 eleven	undici	['unditʃi]
12 twelve	dodici	['doditʃi]
13 thirteen	tredici	['treditʃi]
14 fourteen	quattordici	[kwat'torditʃi]
15 fifteen	quindici	['kwinditʃi]
16 sixteen	sedici	['seditʃi]
17 seventeen	diciassette	[ditʃas'sette]
18 eighteen	diciotto	[di'tʃotto]
19 nineteen	diciannove	[ditʃan'nove]
20 twenty	venti	['venti]
21 twenty-one	ventuno	[ven'tuno]
22 twenty-two	ventidue	['venti 'due]
23 twenty-three	ventitre	['venti 'tre]
30 thirty	trenta	['trenta]
31 thirty-one	trentuno	[tren'tuno]
32 thirty-two	trentadue	[trenta 'due]
33 thirty-three	trentatre	[trenta 'tre]
40 forty	quaranta	[kwa'ranta]
41 forty-one	quarantuno	[kwa'rant'uno]
42 forty-two	quarantadue	[kwa'ranta 'due]
43 forty-three	quarantatre	[kwa'ranta 'tre]
50 fifty	cinquanta	[tʃin'kwanta]
51 fifty-one	cinquantuno	[tʃin'kwant'uno]
52 fifty-two	cinquantadue	[tʃin'kwanta 'due]
53 fifty-three	cinquantatre	[tʃin'kwanta 'tre]
60 sixty	sessanta	[ses'santa]

61 sixty-one	sessantuno	[sessan'tuno]
62 sixty-two	sessantadue	[ses'santa 'due]
63 sixty-three	sessantatre	[ses'santa 'tre]

70 seventy	settanta	[set'tanta]
71 seventy-one	settantuno	[settan'tuno]
72 seventy-two	settantadue	[set'tanta 'due]
73 seventy-three	settantatre	[set'tanta 'tre]

80 eighty	ottanta	[ot'tanta]
81 eighty-one	ottantuno	[ottan'tuno]
82 eighty-two	ottantadue	[ot'tanta 'due]
83 eighty-three	ottantatre	[ot'tanta 'tre]

90 ninety	novanta	[no'vanta]
91 ninety-one	novantuno	[novan'tuno]
92 ninety-two	novantadue	[no'vanta 'due]
93 ninety-three	novantatre	[no'vanta 'tre]

8. Cardinal numbers. Part 2

100 one hundred	cento	['tʃento]
200 two hundred	duecento	[due'tʃento]
300 three hundred	trecento	[tre'tʃento]
400 four hundred	quattrocento	[kwattro'tʃento]
500 five hundred	cinquecento	[tʃinkwe'tʃento]

600 six hundred	seicento	[sej'tʃento]
700 seven hundred	settecento	[sette'tʃento]
800 eight hundred	ottocento	[otto'tʃento]
900 nine hundred	novecento	[nove'tʃento]

1000 one thousand	mille	['mille]
2000 two thousand	duemila	[due'mila]
3000 three thousand	tremila	[tre'mila]
10000 ten thousand	diecimila	['djetʃi 'mila]
one hundred thousand	centomila	[tʃento'mila]
million	milione (m)	[mi'ljone]
billion	miliardo (m)	[mi'ljardo]

9. Ordinal numbers

first (adj)	primo	['primo]
second (adj)	secondo	[se'kondo]
third (adj)	terzo	['tertso]
fourth (adj)	quarto	['kwarto]
fifth (adj)	quinto	['kwinto]
sixth (adj)	sesto	['sesto]

seventh (adj)	**settimo**	['settimo]
eighth (adj)	**ottavo**	[ot'tavo]
ninth (adj)	**nono**	['nono]
tenth (adj)	**decimo**	['detʃimo]

COLOURS. UNITS OF MEASUREMENT

T&P Books Publishing

10. Colors

color	**colore** (m)	[ko'lore]
shade (tint)	**sfumatura** (f)	[sfuma'tura]
hue	**tono** (m)	['tono]
rainbow	**arcobaleno** (m)	[arkoba'leno]
white (adj)	**bianco**	['bjanko]
black (adj)	**nero**	['nero]
gray (adj)	**grigio**	['gridʒo]
green (adj)	**verde**	['verde]
yellow (adj)	**giallo**	['dʒallo]
red (adj)	**rosso**	['rosso]
blue (adj)	**blu**	['blu]
light blue (adj)	**azzurro**	[ad'dzurro]
pink (adj)	**rosa**	['roza]
orange (adj)	**arancione**	[aran'tʃone]
violet (adj)	**violetto**	[vio'letto]
brown (adj)	**marrone**	[mar'rone]
golden (adj)	**d'oro**	['doro]
silvery (adj)	**argenteo**	[ar'dʒenteo]
beige (adj)	**beige**	[beʒ]
cream (adj)	**color crema**	[ko'lor 'krema]
turquoise (adj)	**turchese**	[tur'keze]
cherry red (adj)	**rosso ciliegia** (f)	['rosso tʃi'ljedʒa]
lilac (adj)	**lilla**	['lilla]
crimson (adj)	**rosso lampone**	['rosso lam'pone]
light (adj)	**chiaro**	['kjaro]
dark (adj)	**scuro**	['skuro]
bright, vivid (adj)	**vivo, vivido**	['vivo], ['vivido]
colored (pencils)	**colorato**	[kolo'rato]
color (e.g., ~ film)	**a colori**	[a ko'lori]
black-and-white (adj)	**bianco e nero**	['bjanko e 'nero]
plain (one-colored)	**in tinta unita**	[in 'tinta u'nita]
multicolored (adj)	**multicolore**	[multiko'lore]

11. Units of measurement

weight	**peso** (m)	['pezo]
length	**lunghezza** (f)	[lun'gettsa]

width	larghezza (f)	[lar'gettsa]
height	altezza (f)	[al'tettsa]
depth	profondità (f)	[profondi'ta]
volume	volume (m)	[vo'lume]
area	area (f)	['area]

gram	grammo (m)	['grammo]
milligram	milligrammo (m)	[milli'grammo]
kilogram	chilogrammo (m)	[kilo'grammo]
ton	tonnellata (f)	[tonnel'lata]
pound	libbra (f)	['libbra]
ounce	oncia (f)	['ontʃa]

meter	metro (m)	['metro]
millimeter	millimetro (m)	[mil'limetro]
centimeter	centimetro (m)	[tʃen'timetro]
kilometer	chilometro (m)	[ki'lometro]
mile	miglio (m)	['miʎʎo]

inch	pollice (m)	['pollitʃe]
foot	piede (f)	['pjede]
yard	iarda (f)	[jarda]

square meter	metro (m) quadro	['metro 'kwadro]
hectare	ettaro (m)	['ettaro]
liter	litro (m)	['litro]
degree	grado (m)	['grado]
volt	volt (m)	[volt]
ampere	ampere (m)	[am'pere]
horsepower	cavallo vapore (m)	[ka'vallo va'pore]

quantity	quantità (f)	[kwanti'ta]
a little bit of ...	un po'di ...	[un po di]
half	metà (f)	[me'ta]
dozen	dozzina (f)	[dod'dzina]
piece (item)	pezzo (m)	['pettso]

size	dimensione (f)	[dimen'sjone]
scale (map ~)	scala (f)	['skala]

minimal (adj)	minimo	['minimo]
the smallest (adj)	minore	[mi'nore]
medium (adj)	medio	['medio]
maximal (adj)	massimo	['massimo]
the largest (adj)	maggiore	[ma'dʒore]

12. Containers

canning jar (glass ~)	barattolo (m) di vetro	[ba'rattolo di 'vetro]
can	latta (f), lattina (f)	['latta], [lat'tina]

bucket	**secchio** (m)	['sekkio]
barrel	**barile** (m), **botte** (f)	[ba'rile], ['botte]
wash basin (e.g., plastic ~)	**catino** (m)	[ka'tino]
tank (100L water ~)	**serbatoio** (m)	[serba'tojo]
hip flask	**fiaschetta** (f)	[fias'ketta]
jerrycan	**tanica** (f)	['tanika]
tank (e.g., tank car)	**cisterna** (f)	[tʃi'sterna]
mug	**tazza** (f)	['tattsa]
cup (of coffee, etc.)	**tazzina** (f)	[tat'tsina]
saucer	**piattino** (m)	[pjat'tino]
glass (tumbler)	**bicchiere** (m)	[bik'kjere]
wine glass	**calice** (m)	['kalitʃe]
stock pot (soup pot)	**casseruola** (f)	[kasseru'ola]
bottle (~ of wine)	**bottiglia** (f)	[bot'tiʎʎa]
neck (of the bottle, etc.)	**collo** (m)	['kollo]
carafe (decanter)	**caraffa** (f)	[ka'raffa]
pitcher	**brocca** (f)	['brokka]
vessel (container)	**recipiente** (m)	[retʃi'pjente]
pot (crock, stoneware ~)	**vaso** (m) **di coccio**	['vazo di 'kotʃo]
vase	**vaso** (m)	['vazo]
flacon, bottle (perfume ~)	**boccetta** (f)	[bo'tʃetta]
vial, small bottle	**fiala** (f)	[fi'ala]
tube (of toothpaste)	**tubetto** (m)	[tu'betto]
sack (bag)	**sacco** (m)	['sakko]
bag (paper ~, plastic ~)	**sacchetto** (m)	[sak'ketto]
pack (of cigarettes, etc.)	**pacchetto** (m)	[pak'ketto]
box (e.g., shoebox)	**scatola** (f)	['skatola]
crate	**cassa** (f)	['kassa]
basket	**cesta** (f)	['tʃesta]

MAIN VERBS

T&P Books Publishing

to advise (vt)	consigliare (vt)	[konsiʎ'ʎare]
to agree (say yes)	essere d'accordo	['essere dak'kordo]
to answer (vi, vt)	rispondere (vi, vt)	[ris'pondere]
to apologize (vi)	scusarsi (vr)	[sku'zarsi]
to arrive (vi)	arrivare (vi)	[arri'vare]
to ask (~ oneself)	chiedere, domandare	['kjedere], [doman'dare]
to ask (~ sb to do sth)	chiedere, domandare	['kjedere], [doman'dare]
to be (vi)	essere (vi)	['essere]
to be afraid	avere paura	[a'vere pa'ura]
to be hungry	avere fame	[a'vere 'fame]
to be interested in ...	interessarsi di ...	[interes'sarsi di]
to be needed	occorrere	[ok'korrere]
to be surprised	stupirsi (vr)	[stu'pirsi]
to be thirsty	avere sete	[a'vere 'sete]
to begin (vt)	cominciare (vt)	[komin'tʃare]
to belong to ...	appartenere (vi)	[apparte'nere]
to boast (vi)	vantarsi (vr)	[van'tarsi]
to break (split into pieces)	rompere (vt)	['rompere]
to call (~ for help)	chiamare (vt)	[kja'mare]
can (v aux)	potere (v aus)	[po'tere]
to catch (vt)	afferrare (vt)	[affer'rare]
to change (vt)	cambiare (vt)	[kam'bjare]
to choose (select)	scegliere (vt)	['ʃeʎʎere]
to come down (the stairs)	scendere (vi)	['ʃendere]
to compare (vt)	comparare (vt)	[kompa'rare]
to complain (vi, vt)	lamentarsi (vr)	[lamen'tarsi]
to confuse (mix up)	confondere (vt)	[kon'fondere]
to continue (vt)	continuare (vt)	[kontinu'are]
to control (vt)	controllare (vt)	[kontrol'lare]
to cook (dinner)	cucinare (vi)	[kutʃi'nare]
to cost (vt)	costare (vt)	[ko'stare]
to count (add up)	contare (vt)	[kon'tare]
to count on ...	contare su ...	[kon'tare su]
to create (vt)	creare (vt)	[kre'are]
to cry (weep)	piangere (vi)	['pjandʒere]

14. The most important verbs. Part 2

to deceive (vi, vt)	ingannare (vt)	[ingan'nare]
to decorate (tree, street)	decorare (vt)	[deko'rare]
to defend (a country, etc.)	difendere (vt)	[di'fendere]
to demand (request firmly)	esigere (vt)	[e'ziʤere]
to dig (vt)	scavare (vt)	[ska'vare]

to discuss (vt)	discutere (vt)	[di'skutere]
to do (vt)	fare (vt)	['fare]
to doubt (have doubts)	dubitare (vi)	[dubi'tare]
to drop (let fall)	lasciar cadere	[la'ʃar ka'dere]
to enter (room, house, etc.)	entrare (vi)	[en'trare]

to excuse (forgive)	battaglia (f)	[bat'taʎʎa]
to exist (vi)	esistere (vi)	[e'zistere]
to expect (foresee)	prevedere (vt)	[preve'dere]

to explain (vt)	spiegare (vt)	[spje'gare]
to fall (vi)	cadere (vi)	[ka'dere]

to find (vt)	trovare (vt)	[tro'vare]
to finish (vt)	finire (vt)	[fi'nire]
to fly (vi)	volare (vi)	[vo'lare]

to follow ... (come after)	seguire (vt)	[se'gwire]
to forget (vi, vt)	dimenticare (vt)	[dimenti'kare]

to forgive (vt)	perdonare (vt)	[perdo'nare]
to give (vt)	dare (vt)	['dare]

to give a hint	dare un suggerimento	[dare un suʤeri'mento]
to go (on foot)	andare (vi)	[an'dare]

to go for a swim	fare il bagno	['fare il 'baɲo]
to go out (for dinner, etc.)	uscire (vi)	[u'ʃire]
to guess (the answer)	indovinare (vt)	[indovi'nare]

to have (vt)	avere (vt)	[a'vere]
to have breakfast	fare colazione	['fare kola'tsjone]
to have dinner	cenare (vi)	[ʧe'nare]

to have lunch	pranzare (vi)	[pran'tsare]
to hear (vt)	sentire (vt)	[sen'tire]

to help (vt)	aiutare (vt)	[aju'tare]
to hide (vt)	nascondere (vt)	[na'skondere]
to hope (vi, vt)	sperare (vi, vt)	[spe'rare]
to hunt (vi, vt)	cacciare (vt)	[ka'ʧare]
to hurry (vi)	avere fretta	[a'vere 'fretta]

15. The most important verbs. Part 3

to inform (vt)	informare (vt)	[infor'mare]
to insist (vi, vt)	insistere (vi)	[in'sistere]
to insult (vt)	insultare (vt)	[insul'tare]
to invite (vt)	invitare (vt)	[invi'tare]
to joke (vi)	scherzare (vi)	[sker'tsare]
to keep (vt)	conservare (vt)	[konser'vare]
to keep silent, to hush	tacere (vi)	[ta'tʃere]
to kill (vt)	uccidere (vt)	[u'tʃidere]
to know (sb)	conoscere	[ko'noʃere]
to know (sth)	sapere (vt)	[sa'pere]
to laugh (vi)	ridere (vi)	['ridere]
to liberate (city, etc.)	liberare (vt)	[libe'rare]
to like (I like …)	piacere (vi)	[pja'tʃere]
to look for … (search)	cercare (vt)	[tʃer'kare]
to love (sb)	amare qn	[a'mare]
to make a mistake	sbagliare (vi)	[zbaʎ'ʎare]
to manage, to run	dirigere (vt)	[di'ridʒere]
to mean (signify)	significare (vt)	[siɲifi'kare]
to mention (talk about)	menzionare (vt)	[mentsjo'nare]
to miss (school, etc.)	mancare le lezioni	[man'kare le le'tsjoni]
to notice (see)	accorgersi (vr)	[ak'kordʒersi]
to object (vi, vt)	obiettare (vt)	[objet'tare]
to observe (see)	osservare (vt)	[osser'vare]
to open (vt)	aprire (vt)	[a'prire]
to order (meal, etc.)	ordinare (vt)	[ordi'nare]
to order (mil.)	ordinare (vt)	[ordi'nare]
to own (possess)	possedere (vt)	[posse'dere]
to participate (vi)	partecipare (vi)	[partetʃi'pare]
to pay (vi, vt)	pagare (vi, vt)	[pa'gare]
to permit (vt)	permettere (vt)	[per'mettere]
to plan (vt)	pianificare (vt)	[pjanifi'kare]
to play (children)	giocare (vi)	[dʒo'kare]
to pray (vi, vt)	pregare (vi, vt)	[pre'gare]
to prefer (vt)	preferire (vt)	[prefe'rire]
to promise (vt)	promettere (vt)	[pro'mettere]
to pronounce (vt)	pronunciare (vt)	[pronun'tʃare]
to propose (vt)	proporre (vt)	[pro'porre]
to punish (vt)	punire (vt)	[pu'nire]

16. The most important verbs. Part 4

to read (vi, vt)	leggere (vi, vt)	['ledʒere]
to recommend (vt)	raccomandare (vt)	[rakkoman'dare]

to refuse (vi, vt)	**rifiutarsi** (vr)	[rifju'tarsi]
to regret (be sorry)	**rincrescere** (vi)	[rin'kreʃere]
to rent (sth from sb)	**affittare** (vt)	[affit'tare]
to repeat (say again)	**ripetere** (vt)	[ri'petere]
to reserve, to book	**riservare** (vt)	[rizer'vare]
to run (vi)	**correre** (vi)	['korrere]
to save (rescue)	**salvare** (vt)	[sal'vare]
to say (~ thank you)	**dire** (vt)	['dire]
to scold (vt)	**sgridare** (vt)	[zgri'dare]
to see (vt)	**vedere** (vt)	[ve'dere]
to sell (vt)	**vendere** (vt)	['vendere]
to send (vt)	**mandare** (vt)	[man'dare]
to shoot (vi)	**sparare** (vi)	[spa'rare]
to shout (vi)	**gridare** (vi)	[gri'dare]
to show (vt)	**mostrare** (vt)	[mo'strare]
to sign (document)	**firmare** (vt)	[fir'mare]
to sit down (vi)	**sedersi** (vr)	[se'dersi]
to smile (vi)	**sorridere** (vi)	[sor'ridere]
to speak (vi, vt)	**parlare** (vi, vt)	[par'lare]
to steal (money, etc.)	**rubare** (vt)	[ru'bare]
to stop (for pause, etc.)	**fermarsi** (vr)	[fer'marsi]
to stop (please ~ calling me)	**cessare** (vt)	[tʃes'sare]
to study (vt)	**studiare** (vt)	[stu'djare]
to swim (vi)	**nuotare** (vi)	[nuo'tare]
to take (vt)	**prendere** (vt)	['prendere]
to think (vi, vt)	**pensare** (vi, vt)	[pen'sare]
to threaten (vt)	**minacciare** (vt)	[mina'tʃare]
to touch (with hands)	**toccare** (vt)	[tok'kare]
to translate (vt)	**tradurre** (vt)	[tra'durre]
to trust (vt)	**fidarsi** (vr)	[fi'darsi]
to try (attempt)	**tentare** (vt)	[ten'tare]
to turn (e.g., ~ left)	**girare** (vi)	[dʒi'rare]
to underestimate (vt)	**sottovalutare** (vt)	[sottovalu'tare]
to understand (vt)	**capire** (vt)	[ka'pire]
to unite (vt)	**unire** (vt)	[u'nire]
to wait (vt)	**aspettare** (vt)	[aspet'tare]
to want (wish, desire)	**volere** (vt)	[vo'lere]
to warn (vt)	**avvertire** (vt)	[avver'tire]
to work (vi)	**lavorare** (vi)	[lavo'rare]
to write (vt)	**scrivere** (vt)	['skrivere]
to write down	**annotare** (vt)	[anno'tare]

TIME. CALENDAR

T&P Books Publishing

17. Weekdays

Monday	**lunedì** (m)	[lune'di]
Tuesday	**martedì** (m)	[marte'di]
Wednesday	**mercoledì** (m)	[merkole'di]
Thursday	**giovedì** (m)	[dʒove'di]
Friday	**venerdì** (m)	[vener'di]
Saturday	**sabato** (m)	['sabato]
Sunday	**domenica** (f)	[do'menika]
today (adv)	**oggi**	['odʒi]
tomorrow (adv)	**domani**	[do'mani]
the day after tomorrow	**dopodomani**	[dopodo'mani]
yesterday (adv)	**ieri**	['jeri]
the day before yesterday	**l'altro ieri**	['laltro 'jeri]
day	**giorno** (m)	['dʒorno]
working day	**giorno** (m) **lavorativo**	['dʒorno lavora'tivo]
public holiday	**giorno** (m) **festivo**	['dʒorno fes'tivo]
day off	**giorno** (m) **di riposo**	['dʒorno di ri'pozo]
weekend	**fine** (m) **settimana**	['fine setti'mana]
all day long	**tutto il giorno**	['tutto il 'dʒorno]
the next day (adv)	**l'indomani**	[lindo'mani]
two days ago	**due giorni fa**	['due 'dʒorni fa]
the day before	**il giorno prima**	[il 'dʒorno 'prima]
daily (adj)	**quotidiano**	[kwoti'djano]
every day (adv)	**ogni giorno**	['oɲi 'dʒorno]
week	**settimana** (f)	[setti'mana]
last week (adv)	**la settimana scorsa**	[la setti'mana 'skorsa]
next week (adv)	**la settimana prossima**	[la setti'mana 'prossima]
weekly (adj)	**settimanale**	[settima'nale]
every week (adv)	**ogni settimana**	['oɲi setti'mana]
twice a week	**due volte alla settimana**	['due 'volte 'alla setti'mana]
every Tuesday	**ogni martedì**	['oɲi marte'di]

18. Hours. Day and night

morning	**mattina** (f)	[mat'tina]
in the morning	**di mattina**	[di mat'tina]
noon, midday	**mezzogiorno** (m)	[meddzo'dʒorno]
in the afternoon	**nel pomeriggio**	[nel pome'ridʒo]

evening	sera (f)	['sera]
in the evening	di sera	[di 'sera]
night	notte (f)	['notte]
at night	di notte	[di 'notte]
midnight	mezzanotte (f)	[meddza'notte]

second	secondo (m)	[se'kondo]
minute	minuto (m)	[mi'nuto]
hour	ora (f)	['ora]
half an hour	mezzora (f)	[med'dzora]
a quarter-hour	un quarto d'ora	[un 'kwarto 'dora]
fifteen minutes	quindici minuti	['kwinditʃi mi'nuti]
24 hours	ventiquattro ore	[venti'kwattro 'ore]

sunrise	levata (f) del sole	[le'vata del 'sole]
dawn	alba (f)	['alba]
early morning	mattutino (m)	[mattu'tino]
sunset	tramonto (m)	[tra'monto]

early in the morning	di buon mattino	[di bu'on mat'tino]
this morning	stamattina	[stamat'tina]
tomorrow morning	domattina	[domat'tina]

this afternoon	oggi pomeriggio	['odʒi pome'ridʒo]
in the afternoon	nel pomeriggio	[nel pome'ridʒo]
tomorrow afternoon	domani pomeriggio	[do'mani pome'ridʒo]

| tonight (this evening) | stasera | [sta'sera] |
| tomorrow night | domani sera | [do'mani 'sera] |

at 3 o'clock sharp	alle tre precise	['alle tre pre'tʃize]
about 4 o'clock	verso le quattro	['verso le 'kwattro]
by 12 o'clock	per le dodici	[per le 'doditʃi]

in 20 minutes	fra venti minuti	[fra 'venti mi'nuti]
in an hour	fra un'ora	[fra un 'ora]
on time (adv)	puntualmente	[puntual'mente]

a quarter to …	un quarto di …	[un 'kwarto di]
within an hour	entro un'ora	['entro un 'ora]
every 15 minutes	ogni quindici minuti	['oɲi 'kwinditʃi mi'nuti]
round the clock	giorno e notte	['dʒorno e 'notte]

19. Months. Seasons

January	gennaio (m)	[dʒen'najo]
February	febbraio (m)	[feb'brajo]
March	marzo (m)	['martso]
April	aprile (m)	[a'prile]
May	maggio (m)	['madʒo]

June	giugno (m)	['dʒuɲo]
July	luglio (m)	['luʎʎo]
August	agosto (m)	[a'gosto]
September	settembre (m)	[set'tembre]
October	ottobre (m)	[ot'tobre]
November	novembre (m)	[no'vembre]
December	dicembre (m)	[di'tʃembre]
spring	primavera (f)	[prima'vera]
in spring	in primavera	[in prima'vera]
spring (as adj)	primaverile	[primave'rile]
summer	estate (f)	[e'state]
in summer	in estate	[in e'state]
summer (as adj)	estivo	[e'stivo]
fall	autunno (m)	[au'tunno]
in fall	in autunno	[in au'tunno]
fall (as adj)	autunnale	[autun'nale]
winter	inverno (m)	[in'verno]
in winter	in inverno	[in in'verno]
winter (as adj)	invernale	[inver'nale]
month	mese (m)	['meze]
this month	questo mese	['kwesto 'meze]
next month	il mese prossimo	[il 'meze 'prossimo]
last month	il mese scorso	[il 'meze 'skorso]
a month ago	un mese fa	[un 'meze fa]
in a month (a month later)	fra un mese	[fra un 'meze]
in 2 months (2 months later)	fra due mesi	[fra 'due 'mezi]
the whole month	un mese intero	[un 'meze in'tero]
all month long	per tutto il mese	[per 'tutto il 'meze]
monthly (~ magazine)	mensile	[men'sile]
monthly (adv)	mensilmente	[mensil'mente]
every month	ogni mese	['oɲi 'meze]
twice a month	due volte al mese	['due 'volte al 'meze]
year	anno (m)	['anno]
this year	quest'anno	[kwest'anno]
next year	l'anno prossimo	['lanno 'prossimo]
last year	l'anno scorso	['lanno 'skorso]
a year ago	un anno fa	[un 'anno fa]
in a year	fra un anno	[fra un 'anno]
in two years	fra due anni	[fra 'due 'anni]
the whole year	un anno intero	[un 'anno in'tero]
all year long	per tutto l'anno	[per 'tutto 'lanno]
every year	ogni anno	['oɲi 'anno]

annual (adj)	annuale	[annu'ale]
annually (adv)	annualmente	[annual'mente]
4 times a year	quattro volte all'anno	['kwattro 'volte all 'anno]

date (e.g., today's ~)	data (f)	['data]
date (e.g., ~ of birth)	data (f)	['data]
calendar	calendario (m)	[kalen'dario]

half a year	mezz'anno (m)	[med'dzanno]
six months	semestre (m)	[se'mestre]
season (summer, etc.)	stagione (f)	[sta'dʒone]
century	secolo (m)	['sekolo]

T&P BOOKS

TRAVEL. HOTEL

T&P Books Publishing

20. Trip. Travel

tourism, travel	**turismo** (m)	[tu'rizmo]
tourist	**turista** (m)	[tu'rista]
trip, voyage	**viaggio** (m)	['vjadʒo]
adventure	**avventura** (f)	[avven'tura]
trip, journey	**viaggio** (m)	['vjadʒo]
vacation	**vacanza** (f)	[va'kantsa]
to be on vacation	**essere in vacanza**	['essere in va'kantsa]
rest	**riposo** (m)	[ri'pozo]
train	**treno** (m)	['treno]
by train	**in treno**	[in 'treno]
airplane	**aereo** (m)	[a'ereo]
by airplane	**in aereo**	[in a'ereo]
by car	**in macchina**	[in 'makkina]
by ship	**in nave**	[in 'nave]
luggage	**bagaglio** (m)	[ba'gaʎʎo]
suitcase	**valigia** (f)	[va'lidʒa]
luggage cart	**carrello** (m)	[kar'rello]
passport	**passaporto** (m)	[passa'porto]
visa	**visto** (m)	['visto]
ticket	**biglietto** (m)	[biʎ'ʎetto]
air ticket	**biglietto** (m) **aereo**	[biʎ'ʎetto a'ereo]
guidebook	**guida** (f)	['gwida]
map (tourist ~)	**carta** (f) **geografica**	['karta dʒeo'grafika]
area (rural ~)	**località** (f)	[lokali'ta]
place, site	**luogo** (m)	[lu'ogo]
exotica (n)	**ogetti** (m pl) **esotici**	[o'dʒetti e'zotiʧi]
exotic (adj)	**esotico**	[e'zotiko]
amazing (adj)	**sorprendente**	[sorpren'dente]
group	**gruppo** (m)	['gruppo]
excursion, sightseeing tour	**escursione** (f)	[eskur'sjone]
guide (person)	**guida** (f)	['gwida]

21. Hotel

hotel	**albergo, hotel** (m)	[al'bergo], [o'tel]
motel	**motel** (m)	[mo'tel]

three-star (~ hotel)	tre stelle	[tre 'stelle]
five-star	cinque stelle	['tʃinkwe 'stelle]
to stay (in a hotel, etc.)	alloggiare (vi)	[allo'dʒare]
room	camera (f)	['kamera]
single room	camera (f) singola	['kamera 'singola]
double room	camera (f) doppia	['kamera 'doppia]
to book a room	prenotare una camera	[preno'tare 'una 'kamera]
half board	mezza pensione (f)	['meddza pen'sjone]
full board	pensione (f) completa	[pen'sjone kom'pleta]
with bath	con bagno	[kon 'baɲo]
with shower	con doccia	[kon 'dotʃa]
satellite television	televisione (f) satellitare	[televi'zjone satelli'tare]
air-conditioner	condizionatore (m)	[konditsiona'tore]
towel	asciugamano (m)	[aʃuga'mano]
key	chiave (f)	['kjave]
administrator	amministratore (m)	[amministra'tore]
chambermaid	cameriera (f)	[kame'rjera]
porter, bellboy	portabagagli (m)	[porta·ba'gaʎʎi]
doorman	portiere (m)	[por'tjere]
restaurant	ristorante (m)	[risto'rante]
pub, bar	bar (m)	[bar]
breakfast	colazione (f)	[kola'tsjone]
dinner	cena (f)	['tʃena]
buffet	buffet (m)	[buf'fe]
lobby	hall (f)	[oll]
elevator	ascensore (m)	[aʃen'sore]
DO NOT DISTURB	NON DISTURBARE	[non distur'bare]
NO SMOKING	VIETATO FUMARE!	[vje'tato fu'mare]

22. Sightseeing

monument	monumento (m)	[monu'mento]
fortress	fortezza (f)	[for'tettsa]
palace	palazzo (m)	[pa'lattso]
castle	castello (m)	[ka'stello]
tower	torre (f)	['torre]
mausoleum	mausoleo (m)	[mauzo'leo]
architecture	architettura (f)	[arkitet'tura]
medieval (adj)	medievale	[medje'vale]
ancient (adj)	antico	[an'tiko]
national (adj)	nazionale	[natsio'nale]
famous (monument, etc.)	famoso	[fa'mozo]

tourist	**turista** (m)	[tu'rista]
guide (person)	**guida** (f)	['gwida]
excursion, sightseeing tour	**escursione** (f)	[eskur'sjone]
to show (vt)	**fare vedere**	['fare ve'dere]
to tell (vt)	**raccontare** (vt)	[rakkon'tare]
to find (vt)	**trovare** (vt)	[tro'vare]
to get lost (lose one's way)	**perdersi** (vr)	['perdersi]
map (e.g., subway ~)	**mappa** (f)	['mappa]
map (e.g., city ~)	**piantina** (f)	[pjan'tina]
souvenir, gift	**souvenir** (m)	[suve'nir]
gift shop	**negozio** (m) **di articoli da regalo**	[ne'gotsio di ar'tikoli da re'galo]
to take pictures	**fare foto**	['fare 'foto]
to have one's picture taken	**fotografarsi**	[fotogra'farsi]

T&P BOOKS

TRANSPORTATION

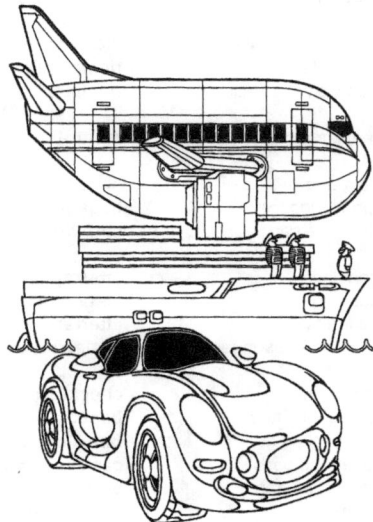

T&P Books Publishing

23. Airport

airport	aeroporto (m)	[aero'porto]
airplane	aereo (m)	[a'ereo]
airline	compagnia (f) aerea	[kompa'ɲia a'erea]
air traffic controller	controllore (m) di volo	[kontrol'lore di 'volo]
departure	partenza (f)	[par'tentsa]
arrival	arrivo (m)	[ar'rivo]
to arrive (by plane)	arrivare (vi)	[arri'vare]
departure time	ora (f) di partenza	['ora di par'tentsa]
arrival time	ora (f) di arrivo	['ora di ar'rivo]
to be delayed	essere ritardato	['essere ritar'dato]
flight delay	volo (m) ritardato	['volo ritar'dato]
information board	tabellone (m) orari	[tabel'lone o'rari]
information	informazione (f)	[informa'tsjone]
to announce (vt)	annunciare (vt)	[annun'tʃare]
flight (e.g., next ~)	volo (m)	['volo]
customs	dogana (f)	[do'gana]
customs officer	doganiere (m)	[doga'njere]
customs declaration	dichiarazione (f)	[dikjara'tsjone]
to fill out (vt)	riempire (vt)	[riem'pire]
to fill out the declaration	riempire una dichiarazione	[riem'pire 'una dikjara'tsjone]
passport control	controllo (m) passaporti	[kon'trollo passa'porti]
luggage	bagaglio (m)	[ba'gaʎʎo]
hand luggage	bagaglio (m) a mano	[ba'gaʎʎo a 'mano]
luggage cart	carrello (m)	[kar'rello]
landing	atterraggio (m)	[atter'radʒo]
landing strip	pista (f) di atterraggio	['pista di atter'radʒo]
to land (vi)	atterrare (vi)	[atter'rare]
airstair (passenger stair)	scaletta (f) dell'aereo	[ska'letta dell a'ereo]
check-in	check-in (m)	[tʃek-in]
check-in counter	banco (m) del check-in	['banko del tʃek-in]
to check-in (vi)	fare il check-in	['fare il tʃek-in]
boarding pass	carta (f) d'imbarco	['karta dim'barko]
departure gate	porta (f) d'imbarco	['porta dim'barko]
transit	transito (m)	['tranzito]

to wait (vt)	aspettare (vt)	[aspet'tare]
departure lounge	sala (f) d'attesa	['sala dat'teza]
to see off	accompagnare (vt)	[akkompa'ɲare]
to say goodbye	congedarsi (vr)	[kondʒe'darsi]

24. Airplane

airplane	aereo (m)	[a'ereo]
air ticket	biglietto (m) aereo	[biʎ'ʎetto a'ereo]
airline	compagnia (f) aerea	[kompa'ɲia a'erea]
airport	aeroporto (m)	[aero'porto]
supersonic (adj)	supersonico	[super'soniko]

captain	comandante (m)	[koman'dante]
crew	equipaggio (m)	[ekwi'padʒo]
pilot	pilota (m)	[pi'lota]
flight attendant (fem.)	hostess (f)	['ostess]
navigator	navigatore (m)	[naviga'tore]

wings	ali (f pl)	['ali]
tail	coda (f)	['koda]
cockpit	cabina (f)	[ka'bina]
engine	motore (m)	[mo'tore]
undercarriage (landing gear)	carrello (m) d'atterraggio	[kar'rello datter'radʒo]
turbine	turbina (f)	[tur'bina]

propeller	elica (f)	['elika]
black box	scatola (f) nera	['skatola 'nera]
yoke (control column)	barra (f) di comando	['barra di ko'mando]
fuel	combustibile (m)	[kombu'stibile]

safety card	safety card (f)	['sejfti kard]
oxygen mask	maschera (f) ad ossigeno	['maskera ad os'sidʒeno]
uniform	uniforme (f)	[uni'forme]
life vest	giubbotto (m) di salvataggio	[dʒub'botto di salva'tadʒo]
parachute	paracadute (m)	[paraka'dute]

takeoff	decollo (m)	[de'kollo]
to take off (vi)	decollare (vi)	[dekol'lare]
runway	pista (f) di decollo	['pista di de'kollo]

visibility	visibilità (f)	[vizibili'ta]
flight (act of flying)	volo (m)	['volo]
altitude	altitudine (f)	[alti'tudine]
air pocket	vuoto (m) d'aria	[vu'oto 'daria]

| seat | posto (m) | ['posto] |
| headphones | cuffia (f) | ['kuffia] |

folding tray (tray table)	tavolinetto (m) pieghevole	[tavoli'netto pje'gevole]
airplane window	oblò (m), finestrino (m)	[ob'lo], [fine'strino]
aisle	corridoio (m)	[korri'dojo]

25. Train

train	treno (m)	['treno]
commuter train	elettrotreno (m)	[elettro'treno]
express train	treno (m) rapido	['treno 'rapido]
diesel locomotive	locomotiva (f) diesel	[lokomo'tiva 'dizel]
steam locomotive	locomotiva (f) a vapore	[lokomo'tiva a va'pore]

| passenger car | carrozza (f) | [kar'rottsa] |
| dining car | vagone (m) ristorante | [va'gone risto'rante] |

rails	rotaie (f pl)	[ro'taje]
railroad	ferrovia (f)	[ferro'via]
railway tie	traversa (f)	[tra'versa]

platform (railway ~)	banchina (f)	[baŋ'kina]
track (~ 1, 2, etc.)	binario (m)	[bi'nario]
semaphore	semaforo (m)	[se'maforo]
station	stazione (f)	[sta'tsjone]

engineer (train driver)	macchinista (m)	[makki'nista]
porter (of luggage)	portabagagli (m)	[porta·ba'gaʎʎi]
car attendant	cuccettista (m, f)	[kutʃet'tista]
passenger	passeggero (m)	[passe'dʒero]
conductor	controllore (m)	[kontrol'lore]
(ticket inspector)		

| corridor (in train) | corridoio (m) | [korri'dojo] |
| emergency brake | freno (m) di emergenza | ['freno di emer'dʒentsa] |

compartment	scompartimento (m)	[skomparti'mento]
berth	cuccetta (f)	[ku'tʃetta]
upper berth	cuccetta (f) superiore	[ku'tʃetta supe'rjore]
lower berth	cuccetta (f) inferiore	[ku'tʃetta infe'rjore]
bed linen, bedding	biancheria (f) da letto	[bjanke'ria da 'letto]

ticket	biglietto (m)	[biʎ'ʎetto]
schedule	orario (m)	[o'rario]
information display	tabellone (m) orari	[tabel'lone o'rari]

to leave, to depart	partire (vi)	[par'tire]
departure (of train)	partenza (f)	[par'tentsa]
to arrive (ab. train)	arrivare (vi)	[arri'vare]
arrival	arrivo (m)	[ar'rivo]
to arrive by train	arrivare con il treno	[arri'vare kon il 'treno]
to get on the train	salire sul treno	[sa'lire sul 'treno]

to get off the train	scendere dal treno	['ʃendere dal 'treno]
train wreck	deragliamento (m)	[deraʎʎa'mento]
to derail (vi)	deragliare (vi)	[deraʎ'ʎare]

steam locomotive	locomotiva (f) a vapore	[lokomo'tiva a va'pore]
stoker, fireman	fuochista (m)	[fo'kista]
firebox	forno (m)	['forno]
coal	carbone (m)	[kar'bone]

26. Ship

| ship | nave (f) | ['nave] |
| vessel | imbarcazione (f) | [imbarka'tsjone] |

steamship	piroscafo (m)	[pi'roskafo]
riverboat	barca (f) fluviale	['barka flu'vjale]
cruise ship	transatlantico (m)	[transat'lantiko]
cruiser	incrociatore (m)	[inkrotʃa'tore]

yacht	yacht (m)	[jot]
tugboat	rimorchiatore (m)	[rimorkja'tore]
barge	chiatta (f)	['kjatta]
ferry	traghetto (m)	[tra'getto]

| sailing ship | veliero (m) | [ve'ljero] |
| brigantine | brigantino (m) | [brigan'tino] |

| ice breaker | rompighiaccio (m) | [rompi'gjatʃo] |
| submarine | sottomarino (m) | [sottoma'rino] |

boat (flat-bottomed ~)	barca (f)	['barka]
dinghy	scialuppa (f)	[ʃa'luppa]
lifeboat	scialuppa (f) di salvataggio	[ʃa'luppa di salva'tadʒo]
motorboat	motoscafo (m)	[moto'skafo]

captain	capitano (m)	[kapi'tano]
seaman	marittimo (m)	[ma'rittimo]
sailor	marinaio (m)	[mari'najo]
crew	equipaggio (m)	[ekwi'padʒo]

boatswain	nostromo (m)	[no'stromo]
ship's boy	mozzo (m) di nave	['mottso di 'nave]
cook	cuoco (m)	[ku'oko]
ship's doctor	medico (m) di bordo	['mediko di 'bordo]

deck	ponte (m)	['ponte]
mast	albero (m)	['albero]
sail	vela (f)	['vela]
hold	stiva (f)	['stiva]

bow (prow)	**prua** (f)	['prua]
stern	**poppa** (f)	['poppa]
oar	**remo** (m)	['remo]
screw propeller	**elica** (f)	['elika]
cabin	**cabina** (f)	[ka'bina]
wardroom	**quadrato** (m) **degli ufficiali**	[kwa'drato 'deʎʎi uffi'tʃali]
engine room	**sala** (f) **macchine**	['sala 'makkine]
bridge	**ponte** (m) **di comando**	['ponte di ko'mando]
radio room	**cabina** (f) **radiotelegrafica**	[ka'bina radiotele'grafika]
wave (radio)	**onda** (f)	['onda]
logbook	**giornale** (m) **di bordo**	[dʒor'nale di 'bordo]
spyglass	**cannocchiale** (m)	[kannok'kjale]
bell	**campana** (f)	[kam'pana]
flag	**bandiera** (f)	[ban'djera]
hawser (mooring ~)	**cavo** (m) **d'ormeggio**	['kavo dor'medʒo]
knot (bowline, etc.)	**nodo** (m)	['nodo]
deckrails	**ringhiera** (f)	[rin'gjera]
gangway	**passerella** (f)	[passe'rella]
anchor	**ancora** (f)	['ankora]
to weigh anchor	**levare l'ancora**	[le'vare 'lankora]
to drop anchor	**gettare l'ancora**	[dʒet'tare 'lankora]
anchor chain	**catena** (f) **dell'ancora**	[ka'tena dell 'ankora]
port (harbor)	**porto** (m)	['porto]
quay, wharf	**banchina** (f)	[baŋ'kina]
to berth (moor)	**ormeggiarsi** (vr)	[orme'dʒarsi]
to cast off	**salpare** (vi)	[sal'pare]
trip, voyage	**viaggio** (m)	['vjadʒo]
cruise (sea trip)	**crociera** (f)	[kro'tʃera]
course (route)	**rotta** (f)	['rotta]
route (itinerary)	**itinerario** (m)	[itine'rario]
fairway (safe water channel)	**tratto** (m) **navigabile**	['tratto navi'gabile]
shallows	**secca** (f)	['sekka]
to run aground	**arenarsi** (vr)	[are'narsi]
storm	**tempesta** (f)	[tem'pesta]
signal	**segnale** (m)	[se'nale]
to sink (vi)	**affondare** (vi)	[affon'dare]
Man overboard!	**Uomo in mare!**	[u'omo in 'mare]
SOS (distress signal)	**SOS**	['esse o 'esse]
ring buoy	**salvagente** (m) **anulare**	[salva'dʒente anu'lare]

T&P BOOKS

CITY

T&P Books Publishing

27. Urban transportation

bus	**autobus** (m)	['autobus]
streetcar	**tram** (m)	[tram]
trolley bus	**filobus** (m)	['filobus]
route (of bus, etc.)	**itinerario** (m)	[itine'rario]
number (e.g., bus ~)	**numero** (m)	['numero]
to go by …	**andare in …**	[an'dare in]
to get on (~ the bus)	**salire su …**	[sa'lire su] .
to get off …	**scendere da …**	['ʃendere da]
stop (e.g., bus ~)	**fermata** (f)	[fer'mata]
next stop	**prossima fermata** (f)	['prossima fer'mata]
terminus	**capolinea** (m)	[kapo'linea]
schedule	**orario** (m)	[o'rario]
to wait (vt)	**aspettare** (vt)	[aspet'tare]
ticket	**biglietto** (m)	[biʎ'ʎetto]
fare	**prezzo** (m) **del biglietto**	['prettso del biʎ'ʎetto]
cashier (ticket seller)	**cassiere** (m)	[kas'sjere]
ticket inspection	**controllo** (m) **dei biglietti**	[kon'trollo dei biʎ'ʎeti]
ticket inspector	**bigliettaio** (m)	[biʎʎet'tajo]
to be late (for …)	**essere in ritardo**	['essere in ri'tardo]
to miss (~ the train, etc.)	**perdere** (vt)	['perdere]
to be in a hurry	**avere fretta**	[a'vere 'fretta]
taxi, cab	**taxi** (m)	['taksi]
taxi driver	**taxista** (m)	[ta'ksista]
by taxi	**in taxi**	[in 'taksi]
taxi stand	**parcheggio** (m) **di taxi**	[par'kedʒo di 'taksi]
to call a taxi	**chiamare un taxi**	[kja'mare un 'taksi]
to take a taxi	**prendere un taxi**	['prendere un 'taksi]
traffic	**traffico** (m)	['traffiko]
traffic jam	**ingorgo** (m)	[in'gorgo]
rush hour	**ore** (f pl) **di punta**	['ore di 'punta]
to park (vi)	**parcheggiarsi** (vr)	[parke'dʒarsi]
to park (vt)	**parcheggiare** (vt)	[parke'dʒare]
parking lot	**parcheggio** (m)	[par'kedʒo]
subway	**metropolitana** (f)	[metropoli'tana]
station	**stazione** (f)	[sta'tsjone]
to take the subway	**prendere la metropolitana**	['prendere la metropoli'tana]

| train | treno (m) | ['treno] |
| train station | stazione (f) ferroviaria | [sta'tsjone ferro'vjaria] |

28. City. Life in the city

city, town	città (f)	[tʃit'ta]
capital city	capitale (f)	[kapi'tale]
village	villaggio (m)	[vil'ladʒo]

city map	mappa (f) della città	['mappa 'della tʃit'ta]
downtown	centro (m) della città	['tʃentro 'della tʃit'ta]
suburb	sobborgo (m)	[sob'borgo]
suburban (adj)	suburbano	[subur'bano]

outskirts	periferia (f)	[perife'ria]
environs (suburbs)	dintorni (m pl)	[din'torni]
city block	isolato (m)	[izo'lato]
residential block (area)	quartiere (m) residenziale	[kwar'tjere reziden'tsjale]

traffic	traffico (m)	['traffiko]
traffic lights	semaforo (m)	[se'maforo]
public transportation	trasporti (m pl) urbani	[tras'porti ur'bani]
intersection	incrocio (m)	[in'krotʃo]

crosswalk	passaggio (m) pedonale	[pas'sadʒo pedo'nale]
pedestrian underpass	sottopassaggio (m)	[sotto·pas'sadʒo]
to cross (~ the street)	attraversare (vt)	[attraver'sare]
pedestrian	pedone (m)	[pe'done]
sidewalk	marciapiede (m)	[martʃa'pjede]

bridge	ponte (m)	['ponte]
embankment (river walk)	banchina (f)	[baŋ'kina]
fountain	fontana (f)	[fon'tana]

allée (garden walkway)	vialetto (m)	[via'letto]
park	parco (m)	['parko]
boulevard	boulevard (m)	[bul'var]
square	piazza (f)	['pjattsa]
avenue (wide street)	viale (m), corso (m)	[vi'ale], ['korso]
street	via (f), strada (f)	['via], ['strada]
side street	vicolo (m)	['vikolo]
dead end	vicolo (m) cieco	['vikolo 'tʃjeko]

house	casa (f)	['kaza]
building	edificio (m)	[edi'fitʃo]
skyscraper	grattacielo (m)	[gratta'tʃelo]

| facade | facciata (f) | [fa'tʃata] |
| roof | tetto (m) | ['tetto] |

window	finestra (f)	[fi'nestra]
arch	arco (m)	['arko]
column	colonna (f)	[ko'lonna]
corner	angolo (m)	['angolo]

store window	vetrina (f)	[ve'trina]
signboard (store sign, etc.)	insegna (f)	[in'seɲa]
poster (e.g., playbill)	cartellone (m)	[kartel'lone]
advertising poster	cartellone (m) pubblicitario	[kartel'lone pubbliʧi'tario]
billboard	tabellone (m) pubblicitario	[tabel'lone pubbliʧi'tario]

garbage, trash	pattume (m), spazzatura (f)	[pat'tume], [spattsa'tura]
trash can (public ~)	pattumiera (f)	[pattu'mjera]
to litter (vi)	sporcare (vi)	[spor'kare]
garbage dump	discarica (f) di rifiuti	[dis'karika di ri'fjuti]

phone booth	cabina (f) telefonica	[ka'bina tele'fonika]
lamppost	lampione (m)	[lam'pjone]
bench (park ~)	panchina (f)	[paŋ'kina]

police officer	poliziotto (m)	[poli'tsjotto]
police	polizia (f)	[poli'tsia]
beggar	mendicante (m)	[mendi'kante]
homeless (n)	barbone (m)	[bar'bone]

29. Urban institutions

store	negozio (m)	[ne'gotsio]
drugstore, pharmacy	farmacia (f)	[farma'ʧia]
eyeglass store	ottica (f)	['ottika]
shopping mall	centro (m) commerciale	['ʧentro kommer'ʧale]
supermarket	supermercato (m)	[supermer'kato]

bakery	panetteria (f)	[panette'ria]
baker	fornaio (m)	[for'najo]
pastry shop	pasticceria (f)	[pastiʧe'ria]
grocery store	drogheria (f)	[droge'ria]
butcher shop	macelleria (f)	[maʧelle'ria]

produce store	fruttivendolo (m)	[frutti'vendolo]
market	mercato (m)	[mer'kato]

coffee house	caffè (m)	[kaf'fe]
restaurant	ristorante (m)	[risto'rante]
pub, bar	birreria (f), pub (m)	[birre'ria], [pab]
pizzeria	pizzeria (f)	[pittse'ria]
hair salon	salone (m) di parrucchiere	[sa'lone di parruk'kjere]

post office	ufficio (m) postale	[uf'fitʃo po'stale]
dry cleaners	lavanderia (f) a secco	[lavande'ria a 'sekko]
photo studio	studio (m) fotografico	['studio foto'grafiko]
shoe store	negozio (m) di scarpe	[ne'gotsio di 'skarpe]
bookstore	libreria (f)	[libre'ria]
sporting goods store	negozio (m) sportivo	[ne'gotsio spor'tivo]
clothes repair shop	riparazione (f) di abiti	[ripara'tsjone di 'abiti]
formal wear rental	noleggio (m) di abiti	[no'ledʒo di 'abiti]
video rental store	noleggio (m) di film	[no'ledʒo di film]
circus	circo (m)	['tʃirko]
zoo	zoo (m)	['dzoo]
movie theater	cinema (m)	['tʃinema]
museum	museo (m)	[mu'zeo]
library	biblioteca (f)	[biblio'teka]
theater	teatro (m)	[te'atro]
opera (opera house)	teatro (m) dell'opera	[te'atro dell 'opera]
nightclub	locale notturno (m)	[lo'kale not'turno]
casino	casinò (m)	[kazi'no]
mosque	moschea (f)	[mos'kea]
synagogue	sinagoga (f)	[sina'goga]
cathedral	cattedrale (f)	[katte'drale]
temple	tempio (m)	['tempjo]
church	chiesa (f)	['kjeza]
college	istituto (m)	[isti'tuto]
university	università (f)	[universi'ta]
school	scuola (f)	['skwola]
prefecture	prefettura (f)	[prefet'tura]
city hall	municipio (m)	[muni'tʃipio]
hotel	albergo (m)	[al'bergo]
bank	banca (f)	['banka]
embassy	ambasciata (f)	[amba'ʃata]
travel agency	agenzia (f) di viaggi	[adʒen'tsia di 'vjadʒi]
information office	ufficio (m) informazioni	[uf'fitʃo informa'tsjoni]
currency exchange	ufficio (m) dei cambi	[uf'fitʃo dei 'kambi]
subway	metropolitana (f)	[metropoli'tana]
hospital	ospedale (m)	[ospe'dale]
gas station	distributore (m) di benzina	[distribu'tore di ben'dzina]
parking lot	parcheggio (m)	[par'kedʒo]

30. Signs

signboard (store sign, etc.)	insegna (f)	[in'sena]
notice (door sign, etc.)	iscrizione (f)	[iskri'tsjone]
poster	cartellone (m)	[kartel'lone]
direction sign	segnale (m) di direzione	[se'nale di dire'tsjone]
arrow (sign)	freccia (f)	['fretʃa]
caution	avvertimento (m)	[avverti'mento]
warning sign	avvertimento (m)	[avverti'mento]
to warn (vt)	avvertire (vt)	[avver'tire]
rest day (weekly ~)	giorno (m) di riposo	['dʒorno di ri'pozo]
timetable (schedule)	orario (m)	[o'rario]
opening hours	orario (m) di apertura	[o'rario di aper'tura]
WELCOME!	BENVENUTI!	[benve'nuti]
ENTRANCE	ENTRATA	[en'trata]
EXIT	USCITA	[u'ʃita]
PUSH	SPINGERE	['spindʒere]
PULL	TIRARE	[ti'rare]
OPEN	APERTO	[a'perto]
CLOSED	CHIUSO	['kjuzo]
WOMEN	DONNE	['donne]
MEN	UOMINI	[u'omini]
DISCOUNTS	SCONTI	['skonti]
SALE	SALDI	['saldi]
NEW!	NOVITÀ!	[novi'ta]
FREE	GRATIS	['gratis]
ATTENTION!	ATTENZIONE!	[atten'tsjone]
NO VACANCIES	COMPLETO	[kom'pleto]
RESERVED	RISERVATO	[rizer'vato]
ADMINISTRATION	AMMINISTRAZIONE	[amministra'tsjone]
STAFF ONLY	RISERVATO AL PERSONALE	[rizer'vato al perso'nale]
BEWARE OF THE DOG!	ATTENTI AL CANE	[at'tenti al 'kane]
NO SMOKING	VIETATO FUMARE!	[vje'tato fu'mare]
DO NOT TOUCH!	NON TOCCARE	[non tok'kare]
DANGEROUS	PERICOLOSO	[periko'lozo]
DANGER	PERICOLO	[pe'rikolo]
HIGH VOLTAGE	ALTA TENSIONE	['alta ten'sjone]
NO SWIMMING!	DIVIETO DI BALNEAZIONE	[di'vjeto di balnea'tsjone]
OUT OF ORDER	GUASTO	['gwasto]

FLAMMABLE   INFIAMMABILE   [infjam'mabile]
FORBIDDEN   VIETATO   [vje'tato]
NO TRESPASSING! VIETATO L'INGRESSO   [vje'tato lin'greso]
WET PAINT   VERNICE FRESCA   [ver'nitʃe 'freska]

31. Shopping

to buy (purchase)	comprare (vt)	[kom'prare]
purchase	acquisto (m)	[a'kwisto]
to go shopping	fare acquisti	['fare a'kwisti]
shopping	shopping (m)	['ʃopping]
to be open (ab. store)	essere aperto	['essere a'perto]
to be closed	essere chiuso	['essere 'kjuzo]
footwear, shoes	calzature (f pl)	[kaltsa'ture]
clothes, clothing	abbigliamento (m)	[abbiʎʎa'mento]
cosmetics	cosmetica (f)	[ko'zmetika]
food products	alimentari (m pl)	[alimen'tari]
gift, present	regalo (m)	[re'galo]
salesman	commesso (m)	[kom'messo]
saleswoman	commessa (f)	[kom'messa]
check out, cash desk	cassa (f)	['kassa]
mirror	specchio (m)	['spekkio]
counter (store ~)	banco (m)	['banko]
fitting room	camerino (m)	[kame'rino]
to try on	provare (vt)	[pro'vare]
to fit (ab. dress, etc.)	stare bene	['stare 'bene]
to like (I like ...)	piacere (vi)	[pja'tʃere]
price	prezzo (m)	['prettso]
price tag	etichetta (f) del prezzo	[eti'ketta del 'prettso]
to cost (vt)	costare (vt)	[ko'stare]
How much?	Quanto?	['kwanto]
discount	sconto (m)	['skonto]
inexpensive (adj)	no muy caro	[no muj 'karo]
cheap (adj)	a buon mercato	[a bu'on mer'kato]
expensive (adj)	caro	['karo]
It's expensive	È caro	[e 'karo]
rental (n)	noleggio (m)	[no'ledʒo]
to rent (~ a tuxedo)	noleggiare (vt)	[nole'dʒare]
credit (trade credit)	credito (m)	['kredito]
on credit (adv)	a credito	[a 'kredito]

CLOTHING & ACCESSORIES

T&P Books Publishing

32. Outerwear. Coats

clothes	vestiti (m pl)	[ve'stiti]
outerwear	soprabito (m)	[so'prabito]
winter clothing	abiti (m pl) invernali	['abiti inver'nali]
coat (overcoat)	cappotto (m)	[kap'potto]
fur coat	pelliccia (f)	[pel'litʃa]
fur jacket	pellicciotto (m)	[pelli'tʃotto]
down coat	piumino (m)	[pju'mino]
jacket (e.g., leather ~)	giubbotto (m), giaccha (f)	[dʒub'botto], ['dʒakka]
raincoat (trenchcoat, etc.)	impermeabile (m)	[imperme'abile]
waterproof (adj)	impermeabile	[imperme'abile]

33. Men's & women's clothing

shirt (button shirt)	camicia (f)	[ka'mitʃa]
pants	pantaloni (m pl)	[panta'loni]
jeans	jeans (m pl)	['dʒins]
suit jacket	giacca (f)	['dʒakka]
suit	abito (m) da uomo	['abito da u'omo]
dress (frock)	abito (m)	['abito]
skirt	gonna (f)	['gonna]
blouse	camicetta (f)	[kami'tʃetta]
knitted jacket (cardigan, etc.)	giacca (f) a maglia	['dʒakka a 'maʎʎa]
jacket (of woman's suit)	giacca (f) tailleur	['dʒakka ta'jer]
T-shirt	maglietta (f)	[maʎ'ʎetta]
shorts (short trousers)	pantaloni (m pl) corti	[panta'loni 'korti]
tracksuit	tuta (f) sportiva	['tuta spor'tiva]
bathrobe	accappatoio (m)	[akkappa'tojo]
pajamas	pigiama (m)	[pi'dʒama]
sweater	maglione (m)	[maʎ'ʎone]
pullover	pullover (m)	[pul'lover]
vest	gilè (m)	[dʒi'le]
tailcoat	frac (m)	[frak]
tuxedo	smoking (m)	['zmoking]
uniform	uniforme (f)	[uni'forme]
workwear	tuta (f) da lavoro	['tuta da la'voro]

| overalls | salopette (f) | [salo'pett] |
| coat (e.g., doctor's smock) | camice (m) | [ka'mitʃe] |

34. Clothing. Underwear

underwear	intimo (m)	['intimo]
boxers, briefs	boxer briefs (m)	['bokser brifs]
panties	mutandina (f)	[mutan'dina]
undershirt (A-shirt)	maglietta (f) intima	[maʎ'ʎetta 'intima]
socks	calzini (m pl)	[kal'tsini]

nightdress	camicia (f) da notte	[ka'mitʃa da 'notte]
bra	reggiseno (m)	[redʒi'seno]
knee highs	calzini (m pl) alti	[kal'tsini 'alti]
(knee-high socks)		
pantyhose	collant (m)	[kol'lant]
stockings (thigh highs)	calze (f pl)	['kaltse]
bathing suit	costume (m) da bagno	[ko'stume da 'baɲo]

35. Headwear

hat	cappello (m)	[kap'pello]
fedora	cappello (m) di feltro	[kap'pello di feltro]
baseball cap	cappello (m) da baseball	[kap'pello da 'bejzbol]
flatcap	coppola (f)	['koppola]

beret	basco (m)	['basko]
hood	cappuccio (m)	[kap'putʃo]
panama hat	panama (m)	['panama]
knit cap (knitted hat)	berretto (m) a maglia	[ber'retto a 'maʎʎa]

| headscarf | fazzoletto (m) da capo | [fattso'letto da 'kapo] |
| women's hat | cappellino (m) donna | [kappel'lino 'donna] |

hard hat	casco (m)	['kasko]
garrison cap	bustina (f)	[bu'stina]
helmet	casco (m)	['kasko]

| derby | bombetta (f) | [bom'betta] |
| top hat | cilindro (m) | [tʃi'lindro] |

36. Footwear

footwear	calzature (f pl)	[kaltsa'ture]
shoes (men's shoes)	stivaletti (m pl)	[stiva'letti]
shoes (women's shoes)	scarpe (f pl)	['skarpe]

| boots (e.g., cowboy ~) | stivali (m pl) | [sti'vali] |
| slippers | pantofole (f pl) | [pan'tofole] |

tennis shoes (e.g., Nike ~)	scarpe (f pl) da tennis	['skarpe da 'tennis]
sneakers	scarpe (f pl) da ginnastica	['skarpe da dʒin'nastika]
(e.g., Converse ~)		
sandals	sandali (m pl)	['sandali]

cobbler (shoe repairer)	calzolaio (m)	[kaltso'lajo]
heel	tacco (m)	['takko]
pair (of shoes)	paio (m)	['pajo]

| shoestring | laccio (m) | ['latʃo] |
| to lace (vt) | allacciare (vt) | [ala'tʃare] |

| shoehorn | calzascarpe (m) | [kaltsa'skarpe] |
| shoe polish | lucido (m) per le scarpe | ['lutʃido per le 'skarpe] |

37. Personal accessories

gloves	guanti (m pl)	['gwanti]
mittens	manopole (f pl)	[ma'nopole]
scarf (muffler)	sciarpa (f)	['ʃarpa]

glasses (eyeglasses)	occhiali (m pl)	[ok'kjali]
frame (eyeglass ~)	montatura (f)	[monta'tura]
umbrella	ombrello (m)	[om'brello]
walking stick	bastone (m)	[ba'stone]

| hairbrush | spazzola (f) per capelli | ['spattsola per ka'pelli] |
| fan | ventaglio (m) | [ven'taʎʎo] |

| tie (necktie) | cravatta (f) | [kra'vatta] |
| bow tie | cravatta (f) a farfalla | [kra'vatta a far'falla] |

| suspenders | bretelle (f pl) | [bre'telle] |
| handkerchief | fazzoletto (m) | [fattso'letto] |

| comb | pettine (m) | ['pettine] |
| barrette | fermaglio (m) | [fer'maʎʎo] |

| hairpin | forcina (f) | [for'tʃina] |
| buckle | fibbia (f) | ['fibbia] |

| belt | cintura (f) | [tʃin'tura] |
| shoulder strap | spallina (f) | [spal'lina] |

bag (handbag)	borsa (f)	['borsa]
purse	borsetta (f)	[bor'setta]
backpack	zaino (m)	['dzajno]

38. Clothing. Miscellaneous

fashion	**moda** (f)	['moda]
in vogue (adj)	**di moda**	[di 'moda]
fashion designer	**stilista** (m)	[sti'lista]

collar	**collo** (m)	['kollo]
pocket	**tasca** (f)	['taska]
pocket (as adj)	**tascabile**	[ta'skabile]
sleeve	**manica** (f)	['manika]
hanging loop	**asola** (f) **per appendere**	['azola per ap'pendere]
fly (on trousers)	**patta** (f)	['patta]

zipper (fastener)	**cerniera** (f) **lampo**	[ʧer'njera 'lampo]
fastener	**chiusura** (f)	[kju'zura]
button	**bottone** (m)	[bot'tone]
buttonhole	**occhiello** (m)	[ok'kjello]
to come off (ab. button)	**staccarsi** (vr)	[stak'karsi]

to sew (vi, vt)	**cucire** (vi, vt)	[ku'ʧire]
to embroider (vi, vt)	**ricamare** (vi, vt)	[rika'mare]
embroidery	**ricamo** (m)	[ri'kamo]
sewing needle	**ago** (m)	['ago]
thread	**filo** (m)	['filo]
seam	**cucitura** (f)	[kuʧi'tura]

to get dirty (vi)	**sporcarsi** (vr)	[spor'karsi]
stain (mark, spot)	**macchia** (f)	['makkia]
to crease, crumple (vi)	**sgualcirsi** (vr)	[zgwal'ʧirsi]
to tear, to rip (vt)	**strappare** (vt)	[strap'pare]
clothes moth	**tarma** (f)	['tarma]

39. Personal care. Cosmetics

toothpaste	**dentifricio** (m)	[denti'friʧo]
toothbrush	**spazzolino** (m) **da denti**	[spatso'lino da 'denti]
to brush one's teeth	**lavarsi i denti**	[la'varsi i 'denti]

razor	**rasoio** (m)	[ra'zojo]
shaving cream	**crema** (f) **da barba**	['krema da 'barba]
to shave (vi)	**rasarsi** (vr)	[ra'zarsi]

soap	**sapone** (m)	[sa'pone]
shampoo	**shampoo** (m)	['ʃampo]

scissors	**forbici** (f pl)	['forbiʧi]
nail file	**limetta** (f)	[li'metta]
nail clippers	**tagliaunghie** (m)	[taʎʎa'ungje]
tweezers	**pinzette** (f pl)	[pin'tsette]

cosmetics	cosmetica (f)	[ko'zmetika]
face mask	maschera (f) di bellezza	['maskera di bel'lettsa]
manicure	manicure (m)	[mani'kure]
to have a manicure	fare la manicure	['fare la mani'kure]
pedicure	pedicure (m)	[pedi'kure]

make-up bag	borsa (f) del trucco	['borsa del 'trukko]
face powder	cipria (f)	['tʃipria]
powder compact	portacipria (m)	[porta·'tʃipria]
blusher	fard (m)	[far]

perfume (bottled)	profumo (m)	[pro'fumo]
toilet water (lotion)	acqua (f) da toeletta	['akwa da toe'letta]
lotion	lozione (f)	[lo'tsjone]
cologne	acqua (f) di Colonia	['akwa di ko'lonia]

eyeshadow	ombretto (m)	[om'bretto]
eyeliner	eyeliner (m)	[aj'lajner]
mascara	mascara (m)	[ma'skara]

lipstick	rossetto (m)	[ros'setto]
nail polish, enamel	smalto (m)	['zmalto]
hair spray	lacca (f) per capelli	['lakka per ka'pelli]
deodorant	deodorante (m)	[deodo'rante]

cream	crema (f)	['krema]
face cream	crema (f) per il viso	['krema per il 'vizo]
hand cream	crema (f) per le mani	['krema per le 'mani]
anti-wrinkle cream	crema (f) antirughe	['krema anti'ruge]
day cream	crema (f) da giorno	['krema da 'dʒorno]
night cream	crema (f) da notte	['krema da 'notte]
day (as adj)	da giorno	[da 'dʒorno]
night (as adj)	da notte	[da 'notte]

tampon	tampone (m)	[tam'pone]
toilet paper (toilet roll)	carta (f) igienica	['karta i'dʒenika]
hair dryer	fon (m)	[fon]

40. Watches. Clocks

watch (wristwatch)	orologio (m)	[oro'lodʒo]
dial	quadrante (m)	[kwa'drante]
hand (of clock, watch)	lancetta (f)	[lan'tʃetta]
metal watch band	braccialetto (m)	[bratʃa'letto]
watch strap	cinturino (m)	[tʃintu'rino]

battery	pila (f)	['pila]
to be dead (battery)	essere scarico	['essere 'skariko]
to change a battery	cambiare la pila	[kam'bjare la 'pila]
to run fast	andare avanti	[an'dare a'vanti]

to run slow	**andare indietro**	[an'dare in'djetro]
wall clock	**orologio** (m) **da muro**	[oro'lodʒo da 'muro]
hourglass	**clessidra** (f)	['klessidra]
sundial	**orologio** (m) **solare**	[oro'lodʒo so'lare]
alarm clock	**sveglia** (f)	['zveʎʎa]
watchmaker	**orologiaio** (m)	[orolo'dʒajo]
to repair (vt)	**riparare** (vt)	[ripa'rare]

T&P BOOKS

EVERYDAY EXPERIENCE

T&P Books Publishing

41. Money

money	soldi (m pl)	['soldi]
currency exchange	cambio (m)	['kambio]
exchange rate	corso (m) di cambio	['korso di 'kambio]
ATM	bancomat (m)	['bankomat]
coin	moneta (f)	[mo'neta]

| dollar | dollaro (m) | ['dollaro] |
| euro | euro (m) | ['euro] |

lira	lira (f)	['lira]
Deutschmark	marco (m)	['marko]
franc	franco (m)	['franko]
pound sterling	sterlina (f)	[ster'lina]
yen	yen (m)	[jen]

debt	debito (m)	['debito]
debtor	debitore (m)	[debi'tore]
to lend (money)	prestare (vt)	[pre'stare]
to borrow (vi, vt)	prendere in prestito	['prendere in 'prestito]

bank	banca (f)	['banka]
account	conto (m)	['konto]
to deposit into the account	versare sul conto	[ver'sare sul 'konto]
to withdraw (vt)	prelevare dal conto	[prele'vare dal 'konto]

credit card	carta (f) di credito	['karta di 'kredito]
cash	contanti (m pl)	[kon'tanti]
check	assegno (m)	[as'seɲo]
to write a check	emettere un assegno	[e'mettere un as'seɲo]
checkbook	libretto (m) di assegni	[li'bretto di as'seɲi]

wallet	portafoglio (m)	[porta·'foʎʎo]
change purse	borsellino (m)	[borsel'lino]
safe	cassaforte (f)	[kassa'forte]

heir	erede (m)	[e'rede]
inheritance	eredità (f)	[eredi'ta]
fortune (wealth)	fortuna (f)	[for'tuna]

lease	affitto (m)	[af'fitto]
rent (money)	affitto (m)	[af'fitto]
to rent (sth from sb)	affittare (vt)	[affit'tare]
price	prezzo (m)	['prettso]
cost	costo (m), prezzo (m)	['kosto], ['prettso]

sum	**somma** (f)	['somma]
to spend (vt)	**spendere** (vt)	['spendere]
expenses	**spese** (f pl)	['speze]
to economize (vi, vt)	**economizzare** (vi, vt)	[ekonomid'dzare]
economical	**economico**	[eko'nomiko]
to pay (vi, vt)	**pagare** (vi, vt)	[pa'gare]
payment	**pagamento** (m)	[paga'mento]
change (give the ~)	**resto** (m)	['resto]
tax	**imposta** (f)	[im'posta]
fine	**multa** (f), **ammenda** (f)	['multa], [am'menda]
to fine (vt)	**multare** (vt)	[mul'tare]

42. Post. Postal service

post office	**posta** (f), **ufficio** (m) **postale**	['posta], [uf'fitʃo po'stale]
mail (letters, etc.)	**posta** (f)	['posta]
mailman	**postino** (m)	[po'stino]
opening hours	**orario** (m) **di apertura**	[o'rario di aper'tura]
letter	**lettera** (f)	['lettera]
registered letter	**raccomandata** (f)	[rakkoman'data]
postcard	**cartolina** (f)	[karto'lina]
telegram	**telegramma** (m)	[tele'gramma]
package (parcel)	**pacco** (m) **postale**	['pakko po'stale]
money transfer	**vaglia** (m) **postale**	['vaʎʎa po'stale]
to receive (vt)	**ricevere** (vt)	[ri'tʃevere]
to send (vt)	**spedire** (vt)	[spe'dire]
sending	**invio** (m)	[in'vio]
address	**indirizzo** (m)	[indi'rittso]
ZIP code	**codice** (m) **postale**	['koditʃe po'stale]
sender	**mittente** (m)	[mit'tente]
receiver	**destinatario** (m)	[destina'tario]
name (first name)	**nome** (m)	['nome]
surname (last name)	**cognome** (m)	[ko'ɲome]
postage rate	**tariffa** (f)	[ta'riffa]
standard (adj)	**ordinario**	[ordi'nario]
economical (adj)	**standard**	['standar]
weight	**peso** (m)	['pezo]
to weigh (~ letters)	**pesare** (vt)	[pe'zare]
envelope	**busta** (f)	['busta]
postage stamp	**francobollo** (m)	[franko'bollo]

43. Banking

| bank | banca (f) | ['banka] |
| branch (of bank, etc.) | filiale (f) | [fi'ljale] |

| bank clerk, consultant | consulente (m) | [konsu'lente] |
| manager (director) | direttore (m) | [diret'tore] |

bank account	conto (m) bancario	['konto ban'kario]
account number	numero (m) del conto	['numero del 'konto]
checking account	conto (m) corrente	['konto kor'rente]
savings account	conto (m) di risparmio	['konto di ris'parmio]

to open an account	aprire un conto	[a'prire un 'konto]
to close the account	chiudere il conto	['kjudere il 'konto]
to deposit into the account	versare sul conto	[ver'sare sul 'konto]
to withdraw (vt)	prelevare dal conto	[prele'vare dal 'konto]
deposit	deposito (m)	[de'pozito]
to make a deposit	depositare (vt)	[depozi'tare]
wire transfer	trasferimento (m) telegrafico	[trasferi'mento tele'grafiko]
to wire, to transfer	rimettere i soldi	[ri'mettere i 'soldi]

| sum | somma (f) | ['somma] |
| How much? | Quanto? | ['kwanto] |

signature	firma (f)	['firma]
to sign (vt)	firmare (vt)	[fir'mare]
credit card	carta (f) di credito	['karta di 'kredito]
code (PIN code)	codice (m)	['koditʃe]
credit card number	numero (m) della carta di credito	['numero 'della 'karta di 'kredito]
ATM	bancomat (m)	['bankomat]

check	assegno (m)	[as'seɲo]
to write a check	emettere un assegno	[e'mettere un as'seɲo]
checkbook	libretto (m) di assegni	[li'bretto di as'seɲi]

loan (bank ~)	prestito (m)	['prestito]
to apply for a loan	fare domanda per un prestito	['fare do'manda per un 'prestito]
to get a loan	ottenere un prestito	[otte'nere un 'prestito]
to give a loan	concedere un prestito	[kon'tʃedere un 'prestito]
guarantee	garanzia (f)	[garan'tsia]

44. Telephone. Phone conversation

| telephone | telefono (m) | [te'lefono] |
| cell phone | telefonino (m) | [telefo'nino] |

answering machine	segreteria (f) telefonica	[segrete'ria tele'fonika]
to call (by phone)	telefonare (vi, vt)	[telefo'nare]
phone call	chiamata (f)	[kja'mata]

to dial a number	comporre un numero	[kom'porre un 'numero]
Hello!	Pronto!	['pronto]
to ask (vt)	chiedere, domandare	['kjedere], [doman'dare]
to answer (vi, vt)	rispondere (vi, vt)	[ris'pondere]

to hear (vt)	udire, sentire (vt)	[u'dire], [sen'tire]
well (adv)	bene	['bene]
not well (adv)	male	['male]
noises (interference)	disturbi (m pl)	[di'sturbi]

receiver	cornetta (f)	[kor'netta]
to pick up (~ the phone)	alzare la cornetta	[al'tsare la kor'netta]
to hang up (~ the phone)	riattaccare la cornetta	[riattak'kare la kor'netta]

busy (engaged)	occupato	[okku'pato]
to ring (ab. phone)	squillare (vi)	[skwil'lare]
telephone book	elenco (m) telefonico	[e'lenko tele'foniko]

local (adj)	locale	[lo'kale]
local call	chiamata (f) locale	[kja'mata lo'kale]
long distance (~ call)	interurbano	[interur'bano]
long-distance call	chiamata (f) interurbana	[kja'mata interur'bana]
international (adj)	internazionale	[internatsjo'nale]
international call	chiamata (f) internazionale	[kja'mata internatsjo'nale]

45. Cell phone

cell phone	telefonino (m)	[telefo'nino]
display	schermo (m)	['skermo]
button	tasto (m)	['tasto]
SIM card	scheda SIM (f)	['skeda 'sim]

battery	pila (f)	['pila]
to be dead (battery)	essere scarico	['essere 'skariko]
charger	caricabatteria (m)	[karika·batte'ria]

menu	menù (m)	[me'nu]
settings	impostazioni (f pl)	[imposta'tsjoni]
tune (melody)	melodia (f)	[melo'dia]
to select (vt)	scegliere (vt)	['ʃeʎʎere]

calculator	calcolatrice (f)	[kalkola'tritʃe]
voice mail	segreteria (f) telefonica	[segrete'ria tele'fonika]
alarm clock	sveglia (f)	['zveʎʎa]
contacts	contatti (m pl)	[kon'tatti]

SMS (text message)	**messaggio** (m) **SMS**	[mes'sadʒo ese'mese]
subscriber	**abbonato** (m)	[abbo'nato]

46. Stationery

ballpoint pen	**penna** (f) **a sfera**	[penna a 'sfera]
fountain pen	**penna** (f) **stilografica**	['penna stilo'grafika]
pencil	**matita** (f)	[ma'tita]
highlighter	**evidenziatore** (m)	[evidentsja'tore]
felt-tip pen	**pennarello** (m)	[penna'rello]
notepad	**taccuino** (m)	[tak'kwino]
agenda (diary)	**agenda** (f)	[a'dʒenda]
ruler	**righello** (m)	[ri'gello]
calculator	**calcolatrice** (f)	[kalkola'tritʃe]
eraser	**gomma** (f) **per cancellare**	['gomma per kantʃel'lare]
thumbtack	**puntina** (f)	[pun'tina]
paper clip	**graffetta** (f)	[graf'fetta]
glue	**colla** (f)	['kolla]
stapler	**pinzatrice** (f)	[pintsa'tritʃe]
hole punch	**perforatrice** (f)	[perfora'tritʃe]
pencil sharpener	**temperamatite** (m)	[temperama'tite]

47. Foreign languages

language	**lingua** (f)	['lingua]
foreign (adj)	**straniero**	[stra'njero]
foreign language	**lingua** (f) **straniera**	['lingua stra'njera]
to study (vt)	**studiare** (vt)	[stu'djare]
to learn (language, etc.)	**imparare** (vt)	[impa'rare]
to read (vi, vt)	**leggere** (vi, vt)	['ledʒere]
to speak (vi, vt)	**parlare** (vi, vt)	[par'lare]
to understand (vt)	**capire** (vt)	[ka'pire]
to write (vt)	**scrivere** (vi, vt)	['skrivere]
fast (adv)	**rapidamente**	[rapida'mente]
slowly (adv)	**lentamente**	[lenta'mente]
fluently (adv)	**correntemente**	[korrente'mente]
rules	**regole** (f pl)	['regole]
grammar	**grammatica** (f)	[gram'matika]
vocabulary	**lessico** (m)	['lessiko]
phonetics	**fonetica** (f)	[fo'netika]
textbook	**manuale** (m)	[manu'ale]

dictionary	dizionario (m)	[ditsjo'nario]
teach-yourself book	manuale (m) autodidattico	[manu'ale autodi'dattiko]
phrasebook	frasario (m)	[fra'zario]
cassette, tape	cassetta (f)	[kas'setta]
videotape	videocassetta (f)	[video·kas'setta]
CD, compact disc	CD (m)	[ʧi'di]
DVD	DVD (m)	[divu'di]
alphabet	alfabeto (m)	[alfa'beto]
to spell (vt)	compitare (vt)	[kompi'tare]
pronunciation	pronuncia (f)	[pro'nunʧa]
accent	accento (m)	[a'ʧento]
with an accent	con un accento	[kon un a'ʧento]
without an accent	senza accento	['sentsa a'ʧento]
word	vocabolo (m)	[vo'kabolo]
meaning	significato (m)	[siɲifi'kato]
course (e.g., a French ~)	corso (m)	['korso]
to sign up	iscriversi (vr)	[is'kriversi]
teacher	insegnante (m, f)	[inse'ɲante]
translation (process)	traduzione (f)	[tradu'tsjone]
translation (text, etc.)	traduzione (f)	[tradu'tsjone]
translator	traduttore (m)	[tradut'tore]
interpreter	interprete (m)	[in'terprete]
polyglot	poliglotta (m)	[poli'glotta]
memory	memoria (f)	[me'moria]

MEALS. RESTAURANT

T&P Books Publishing

48. Table setting

spoon	**cucchiaio** (m)	[kuk'kjajo]
knife	**coltello** (m)	[kol'tello]
fork	**forchetta** (f)	[for'ketta]
cup (e.g., coffee ~)	**tazza** (f)	['tattsa]
plate (dinner ~)	**piatto** (m)	['pjatto]
saucer	**piattino** (m)	[pjat'tino]
napkin (on table)	**tovagliolo** (m)	[tovaʎ'ʎolo]
toothpick	**stuzzicadenti** (m)	[stuttsika'denti]

49. Restaurant

restaurant	**ristorante** (m)	[risto'rante]
coffee house	**caffè** (m)	[kaf'fe]
pub, bar	**pub** (m), **bar** (m)	[pab], [bar]
tearoom	**sala** (f) **da tè**	['sala da 'te]
waiter	**cameriere** (m)	[kame'rjere]
waitress	**cameriera** (f)	[kame'rjera]
bartender	**barista** (m)	[ba'rista]
menu	**menù** (m)	[me'nu]
wine list	**lista** (f) **dei vini**	['lista 'dei 'vini]
to book a table	**prenotare un tavolo**	[preno'tare un 'tavolo]
course, dish	**piatto** (m)	['pjatto]
to order (meal)	**ordinare** (vt)	[ordi'nare]
to make an order	**fare un'ordinazione**	['fare unordina'tsjone]
aperitif	**aperitivo** (m)	[aperi'tivo]
appetizer	**antipasto** (m)	[anti'pasto]
dessert	**dolce** (m)	['doltʃe]
check	**conto** (m)	['konto]
to pay the check	**pagare il conto**	[pa'gare il 'konto]
to give change	**dare il resto**	['dare il 'resto]
tip	**mancia** (f)	['mantʃa]

50. Meals

food	**cibo** (m)	['tʃibo]
to eat (vi, vt)	**mangiare** (vi, vt)	[man'dʒare]

breakfast	colazione (f)	[kola'tsjone]
to have breakfast	fare colazione	['fare kola'tsjone]
lunch	pranzo (m)	['prantso]
to have lunch	pranzare (vi)	[pran'tsare]
dinner	cena (f)	['tʃena]
to have dinner	cenare (vi)	[tʃe'nare]
appetite	appetito (m)	[appe'tito]
Enjoy your meal!	Buon appetito!	[bu'on appe'tito]
to open (~ a bottle)	aprire (vt)	[a'prire]
to spill (liquid)	rovesciare (vt)	[rove'ʃare]
to spill out (vi)	rovesciarsi (vi)	[rove'ʃarsi]
to boil (vi)	bollire (vi)	[bol'lire]
to boil (vt)	far bollire	[far bol'lire]
boiled (~ water)	bollito	[bol'lito]
to chill, cool down (vt)	raffreddare (vt)	[raffred'dare]
to chill (vi)	raffreddarsi (vr)	[raffred'darsi]
taste, flavor	gusto (m)	['gusto]
aftertaste	retrogusto (m)	[retro'gusto]
to slim down (lose weight)	essere a dieta	['essere a di'eta]
diet	dieta (f)	[di'eta]
vitamin	vitamina (f)	[vita'mina]
calorie	caloria (f)	[kalo'ria]
vegetarian (n)	vegetariano (m)	[vedʒeta'rjano]
vegetarian (adj)	vegetariano	[vedʒeta'rjano]
fats (nutrient)	grassi (m pl)	['grassi]
proteins	proteine (f pl)	[prote'ine]
carbohydrates	carboidrati (m pl)	[karboi'drati]
slice (of lemon, ham)	fetta (f), fettina (f)	['fetta], [fet'tina]
piece (of cake, pie)	pezzo (m)	['pettso]
crumb	briciola (f)	['britʃola]
(of bread, cake, etc.)		

51. Cooked dishes

course, dish	piatto (m)	['pjatto]
cuisine	cucina (f)	[ku'tʃina]
recipe	ricetta (f)	[ri'tʃetta]
portion	porzione (f)	[por'tsjone]
salad	insalata (f)	[insa'lata]
soup	minestra (f)	[mi'nestra]
clear soup (broth)	brodo (m)	['brodo]
sandwich (bread)	panino (m)	[pa'nino]

fried eggs	uova (f pl) al tegamino	[u'ova al tega'mino]
hamburger (beefburger)	hamburger (m)	[am'burger]
beefsteak	bistecca (f)	[bi'stekka]

side dish	contorno (m)	[kon'torno]
spaghetti	spaghetti (m pl)	[spa'getti]
mashed potatoes	purè (m) di patate	[pu're di pa'tate]
pizza	pizza (f)	['pittsa]
porridge (oatmeal, etc.)	porridge (m)	[por'ridʒe]
omelet	frittata (f)	[frit'tata]

boiled (e.g., ~ beef)	bollito	[bol'lito]
smoked (adj)	affumicato	[affumi'kato]
fried (adj)	fritto	['fritto]
dried (adj)	secco	['sekko]
frozen (adj)	congelato	[kondʒe'lato]
pickled (adj)	sottoaceto	[sottoa'tʃeto]

sweet (sugary)	dolce	['doltʃe]
salty (adj)	salato	[sa'lato]
cold (adj)	freddo	['freddo]
hot (adj)	caldo	['kaldo]
bitter (adj)	amaro	[a'maro]
tasty (adj)	buono, gustoso	[bu'ono], [gu'stozo]

to cook in boiling water	cuocere, preparare (vt)	[ku'otʃere], [prepa'rare]
to cook (dinner)	cucinare (vi)	[kutʃi'nare]
to fry (vt)	friggere (vt)	['fridʒere]
to heat up (food)	riscaldare (vt)	[riskal'dare]

to salt (vt)	salare (vt)	[sa'lare]
to pepper (vt)	pepare (vt)	[pe'pare]
to grate (vt)	grattugiare (vt)	[grattu'dʒare]
peel (n)	buccia (f)	['butʃa]
to peel (vt)	sbucciare (vt)	[zbu'tʃare]

52. Food

meat	carne (f)	['karne]
chicken	pollo (m)	['pollo]
Rock Cornish hen (poussin)	pollo (m) novello	['pollo no'vello]
duck	anatra (f)	['anatra]
goose	oca (f)	['oka]
game	cacciagione (f)	[katʃa'dʒone]
turkey	tacchino (m)	[tak'kino]

pork	maiale (m)	[ma'jale]
veal	vitello (m)	[vi'tello]
lamb	agnello (m)	[a'ɲello]

| beef | manzo (m) | ['mandzo] |
| rabbit | coniglio (m) | [ko'niʎʎo] |

sausage (bologna, etc.)	salame (m)	[sa'lame]
vienna sausage (frankfurter)	würstel (m)	['vyrstel]
bacon	pancetta (f)	[pan'tʃetta]
ham	prosciutto (m)	[pro'ʃutto]
gammon	prosciutto (m) affumicato	[pro'ʃutto affumi'kato]

pâté	pâté (m)	[pa'te]
liver	fegato (m)	['fegato]
hamburger (ground beef)	carne (f) trita	['karne 'trita]
tongue	lingua (f)	['lingua]

egg	uovo (m)	[u'ovo]
eggs	uova (f pl)	[u'ova]
egg white	albume (m)	[al'bume]
egg yolk	tuorlo (m)	[tu'orlo]

fish	pesce (m)	['peʃe]
seafood	frutti (m pl) di mare	['frutti di 'mare]
crustaceans	crostacei (m pl)	[kro'statʃei]
caviar	caviale (m)	[ka'vjale]

crab	granchio (m)	['graŋkio]
shrimp	gamberetto (m)	[gambe'retto]
oyster	ostrica (f)	['ostrika]
spiny lobster	aragosta (f)	[ara'gosta]
octopus	polpo (m)	['polpo]
squid	calamaro (m)	[kala'maro]

sturgeon	storione (m)	[sto'rjone]
salmon	salmone (m)	[sal'mone]
halibut	ippoglosso (m)	[ippo'glosso]

cod	merluzzo (m)	[mer'luttso]
mackerel	scombro (m)	['skombro]
tuna	tonno (m)	['tonno]
eel	anguilla (f)	[an'gwilla]

trout	trota (f)	['trota]
sardine	sardina (f)	[sar'dina]
pike	luccio (m)	['lutʃo]
herring	aringa (f)	[a'ringa]

bread	pane (m)	['pane]
cheese	formaggio (m)	[for'madʒo]
sugar	zucchero (m)	['dzukkero]
salt	sale (m)	['sale]
rice	riso (m)	['rizo]
pasta (macaroni)	pasta (f)	['pasta]

T&P Books. English-Italian phrasebook & topical vocabulary

noodles	tagliatelle (f pl)	[taʎʎa'telle]
butter	burro (m)	['burro]
vegetable oil	olio (m) vegetale	['oljo vedʒe'tale]
sunflower oil	olio (m) di girasole	['oljo di dʒira'sole]
margarine	margarina (f)	[marga'rina]

| olives | olive (f pl) | [o'live] |
| olive oil | olio (m) d'oliva | ['oljo do'liva] |

milk	latte (m)	['latte]
condensed milk	latte (m) condensato	['latte konden'sato]
yogurt	yogurt (m)	['jogurt]
sour cream	panna (f) acida	['panna 'atʃida]
cream (of milk)	panna (f)	['panna]

| mayonnaise | maionese (m) | [majo'neze] |
| buttercream | crema (f) | ['krema] |

groats (barley ~, etc.)	cereali (m pl)	[tʃere'ali]
flour	farina (f)	[fa'rina]
canned food	cibi (m pl) in scatola	['tʃibi in 'skatola]

cornflakes	fiocchi (m pl) di mais	['fjokki di 'mais]
honey	miele (m)	['mjele]
jam	marmellata (f)	[marmel'lata]
chewing gum	gomma (f) da masticare	['gomma da masti'kare]

53. Drinks

water	acqua (f)	['akwa]
drinking water	acqua (f) potabile	['akwa po'tabile]
mineral water	acqua (f) minerale	['akwa mine'rale]

still (adj)	liscia, non gassata	['liʃa], [non gas'sata]
carbonated (adj)	gassata	[gas'sata]
sparkling (adj)	frizzante	[frid'dzante]
ice	ghiaccio (m)	['gjatʃo]
with ice	con ghiaccio	[kon 'gjatʃo]

non-alcoholic (adj)	analcolico	[anal'koliko]
soft drink	bevanda (f) analcolica	[be'vanda anal'kolika]
refreshing drink	bibita (f)	['bibita]
lemonade	limonata (f)	[limo'nata]

liquors	bevande (f pl) alcoliche	[be'vande al'kolike]
wine	vino (m)	['vino]
white wine	vino (m) bianco	['vino 'bjanko]
red wine	vino (m) rosso	['vino 'rosso]
liqueur	liquore (m)	[li'kwore]
champagne	champagne (m)	[ʃam'paɲ]

140

vermouth	vermouth (m)	['vermut]
whiskey	whisky	['wiski]
vodka	vodka (f)	['vodka]
gin	gin (m)	[dʒin]
cognac	cognac (m)	['koɲak]
rum	rum (m)	[rum]
coffee	caffè (m)	[kaf'fe]
black coffee	caffè (m) nero	[kaf'fe 'nero]
coffee with milk	caffè latte (m)	[kaf'fe 'latte]
cappuccino	cappuccino (m)	[kappu'tʃino]
instant coffee	caffè (m) solubile	[kaf'fe so'lubile]
milk	latte (m)	['latte]
cocktail	cocktail (m)	['koktejl]
milkshake	frullato (m)	[frul'lato]
juice	succo (m)	['sukko]
tomato juice	succo (m) di pomodoro	['sukko di pomo'doro]
orange juice	succo (m) d'arancia	['sukko da'rantʃa]
freshly squeezed juice	spremuta (f)	[spre'muta]
beer	birra (f)	['birra]
light beer	birra (f) chiara	['birra 'kjara]
dark beer	birra (f) scura	['birra 'skura]
tea	tè (m)	[te]
black tea	tè (m) nero	[te 'nero]
green tea	tè (m) verde	[te 'verde]

54. Vegetables

vegetables	ortaggi (m pl)	[or'tadʒi]
greens	verdura (f)	[ver'dura]
tomato	pomodoro (m)	[pomo'doro]
cucumber	cetriolo (m)	[tʃetri'olo]
carrot	carota (f)	[ka'rota]
potato	patata (f)	[pa'tata]
onion	cipolla (f)	[tʃi'polla]
garlic	aglio (m)	['aʎʎo]
cabbage	cavolo (m)	['kavolo]
cauliflower	cavolfiore (m)	[kavol'fjore]
Brussels sprouts	cavoletti (m pl) di Bruxelles	[kavo'letti di bruk'sel]
broccoli	broccolo (m)	['brokkolo]
beet	barbabietola (f)	[barba'bjetola]
eggplant	melanzana (f)	[melan'tsana]

zucchini	zucchina (f)	[dzuk'kina]
pumpkin	zucca (f)	['dzukka]
turnip	rapa (f)	['rapa]

parsley	prezzemolo (m)	[pret'tsemolo]
dill	aneto (m)	[a'neto]
lettuce	lattuga (f)	[lat'tuga]
celery	sedano (m)	['sedano]
asparagus	asparago (m)	[a'sparago]
spinach	spinaci (m pl)	[spi'natʃi]

pea	pisello (m)	[pi'zello]
beans	fave (f pl)	['fave]
corn (maize)	mais (m)	['mais]
kidney bean	fagiolo (m)	[fa'dʒolo]

bell pepper	peperone (m)	[pepe'rone]
radish	ravanello (m)	[rava'nello]
artichoke	carciofo (m)	[kar'tʃofo]

55. Fruits. Nuts

fruit	frutto (m)	['frutto]
apple	mela (f)	['mela]
pear	pera (f)	['pera]
lemon	limone (m)	[li'mone]
orange	arancia (f)	[a'rantʃa]
strawberry (garden ~)	fragola (f)	['fragola]

mandarin	mandarino (m)	[manda'rino]
plum	prugna (f)	['pruɲa]
peach	pesca (f)	['peska]
apricot	albicocca (f)	[albi'kokka]
raspberry	lampone (m)	[lam'pone]
pineapple	ananas (m)	[ana'nas]

banana	banana (f)	[ba'nana]
watermelon	anguria (f)	[an'guria]
grape	uva (f)	['uva]
sour cherry	amarena (f)	[ama'rena]
sweet cherry	ciliegia (f)	[tʃi'ljedʒa]
melon	melone (m)	[me'lone]

grapefruit	pompelmo (m)	[pom'pelmo]
avocado	avocado (m)	[avo'kado]
papaya	papaia (f)	[pa'paja]
mango	mango (m)	['mango]
pomegranate	melagrana (f)	[mela'grana]
redcurrant	ribes (m) rosso	['ribes 'rosso]
blackcurrant	ribes (m) nero	['ribes 'nero]

gooseberry	**uva** (f) **spina**	['uva 'spina]
bilberry	**mirtillo** (m)	[mir'tillo]
blackberry	**mora** (f)	['mora]

raisin	**uvetta** (f)	[u'vetta]
fig	**fico** (m)	['fiko]
date	**dattero** (m)	['dattero]

peanut	**arachide** (f)	[a'rakide]
almond	**mandorla** (f)	['mandorla]
walnut	**noce** (f)	['notʃe]
hazelnut	**nocciola** (f)	[no'tʃola]
coconut	**noce** (f) **di cocco**	['notʃe di 'kokko]
pistachios	**pistacchi** (m pl)	[pi'stakki]

56. Bread. Candy

bakers' confectionery (pastry)	**pasticceria** (f)	[pastitʃe'ria]
bread	**pane** (m)	['pane]
cookies	**biscotti** (m pl)	[bi'skotti]

chocolate (n)	**cioccolato** (m)	[tʃokko'lato]
chocolate (as adj)	**al cioccolato**	[al tʃokko'lato]
candy (wrapped)	**caramella** (f)	[kara'mella]
cake (e.g., cupcake)	**tortina** (f)	[tor'tina]
cake (e.g., birthday ~)	**torta** (f)	['torta]

pie (e.g., apple ~)	**crostata** (f)	[kro'stata]
filling (for cake, pie)	**ripieno** (m)	[ri'pjeno]

jam (whole fruit jam)	**marmellata** (f)	[marmel'lata]
marmalade	**marmellata** (f) **di agrumi**	[marmel'lata di a'grumi]
wafers	**wafer** (m)	['vafer]
ice-cream	**gelato** (m)	[dʒe'lato]
pudding	**budino** (m)	[bu'dino]

57. Spices

salt	**sale** (m)	['sale]
salty (adj)	**salato**	[sa'lato]
to salt (vt)	**salare** (vt)	[sa'lare]

black pepper	**pepe** (m) **nero**	['pepe 'nero]
red pepper (milled ~)	**peperoncino** (m)	[peperon'tʃino]
mustard	**senape** (f)	[se'nape]
horseradish	**cren** (m)	['kren]
condiment	**condimento** (m)	[kondi'mento]

spice	**spezie** (f pl)	['spetsie]
sauce	**salsa** (f)	['salsa]
vinegar	**aceto** (m)	[a'tʃeto]
anise	**anice** (m)	['anitʃe]
basil	**basilico** (m)	[ba'ziliko]
cloves	**chiodi** (m pl) **di garofano**	['kjodi di ga'rofano]
ginger	**zenzero** (m)	['dzendzero]
coriander	**coriandolo** (m)	[kori'andolo]
cinnamon	**cannella** (f)	[kan'nella]
sesame	**sesamo** (m)	[sezamo]
bay leaf	**alloro** (m)	[al'loro]
paprika	**paprica** (f)	['paprika]
caraway	**cumino, comino** (m)	[ku'mino], [ko'mino]
saffron	**zafferano** (m)	[dzaffe'rano]

PERSONAL INFORMATION. FAMILY

T&P Books Publishing

name (first name)	**nome** (m)	['nome]
surname (last name)	**cognome** (m)	[ko'ɲome]
date of birth	**data** (f) **di nascita**	['data di 'naʃita]
place of birth	**luogo** (m) **di nascita**	[lu'ogo di 'naʃita]
nationality	**nazionalità** (f)	[natsjonali'ta]
place of residence	**domicilio** (m)	[domi'tʃilio]
country	**paese** (m)	[pa'eze]
profession (occupation)	**professione** (f)	[profes'sjone]
gender, sex	**sesso** (m)	['sesso]
height	**statura** (f)	[sta'tura]
weight	**peso** (m)	['pezo]

mother	**madre** (f)	['madre]
father	**padre** (m)	['padre]
son	**figlio** (m)	['fiʎʎo]
daughter	**figlia** (f)	['fiʎʎa]
younger daughter	**figlia** (f) **minore**	['fiʎʎa mi'nore]
younger son	**figlio** (m) **minore**	['fiʎʎo mi'nore]
eldest daughter	**figlia** (f) **maggiore**	['fiʎʎa ma'dʒore]
eldest son	**figlio** (m) **maggiore**	['fiʎʎo ma'dʒore]
brother	**fratello** (m)	[fra'tello]
sister	**sorella** (f)	[so'rella]
cousin (masc.)	**cugino** (m)	[ku'dʒino]
cousin (fem.)	**cugina** (f)	[ku'dʒina]
mom, mommy	**mamma** (f)	['mamma]
dad, daddy	**papà** (m)	[pa'pa]
parents	**genitori** (m pl)	[dʒeni'tori]
child	**bambino** (m)	[bam'bino]
children	**bambini** (m pl)	[bam'bini]
grandmother	**nonna** (f)	['nonna]
grandfather	**nonno** (m)	['nonno]
grandson	**nipote** (m)	[ni'pote]
granddaughter	**nipote** (f)	[ni'pote]
grandchildren	**nipoti** (pl)	[ni'poti]

uncle	**zio** (m)	['tsio]
aunt	**zia** (f)	['tsia]
nephew	**nipote** (m)	[ni'pote]
niece	**nipote** (f)	[ni'pote]

mother-in-law (wife's mother)	**suocera** (f)	[su'otʃera]
father-in-law (husband's father)	**suocero** (m)	[su'otʃero]
son-in-law (daughter's husband)	**genero** (m)	['dʒenero]
stepmother	**matrigna** (f)	[ma'triɲa]
stepfather	**patrigno** (m)	[pa'triɲo]

infant	**neonato** (m)	[neo'nato]
baby (infant)	**infante** (m)	[in'fante]
little boy, kid	**bimbo** (m)	['bimbo]

wife	**moglie** (f)	['moʎʎe]
husband	**marito** (m)	[ma'rito]
spouse (husband)	**coniuge** (m)	['konjudʒe]
spouse (wife)	**coniuge** (f)	['konjudʒe]

married (masc.)	**sposato**	[spo'zato]
married (fem.)	**sposata**	[spo'zata]
single (unmarried)	**celibe**	['tʃelibe]
bachelor	**scapolo** (m)	['skapolo]
divorced (masc.)	**divorziato**	[divortsi'ato]
widow	**vedova** (f)	['vedova]
widower	**vedovo** (m)	['vedovo]

relative	**parente** (m)	[pa'rente]
close relative	**parente** (m) **stretto**	[pa'rente 'stretto]
distant relative	**parente** (m) **lontano**	[pa'rente lon'tano]
relatives	**parenti** (m pl)	[pa'renti]

orphan (boy)	**orfano** (m)	['orfano]
orphan (girl)	**orfana** (f)	['orfana]
guardian (of a minor)	**tutore** (m)	[tu'tore]
to adopt (a boy)	**adottare** (vt)	[adot'tare]
to adopt (a girl)	**adottare** (vt)	[adot'tare]

60. Friends. Coworkers

friend (masc.)	**amico** (m)	[a'miko]
friend (fem.)	**amica** (f)	[a'mika]
friendship	**amicizia** (f)	[ami'tʃitsia]
to be friends	**essere amici**	['essere a'mitʃi]
buddy (masc.)	**amico** (m)	[a'miko]
buddy (fem.)	**amica** (f)	[a'mika]

partner	**partner** (m)	['partner]
chief (boss)	**capo** (m)	['kapo]
superior (n)	**capo** (m), **superiore** (m)	['kapo], [supe'rjore]
subordinate (n)	**subordinato** (m)	[subordi'nato]
colleague	**collega** (m)	[kol'lega]
acquaintance (person)	**conoscente** (m)	[kono'ʃente]
fellow traveler	**compagno** (m) **di viaggio**	[kom'paɲo di 'vjadʒo]
classmate	**compagno** (m) **di classe**	[kom'paɲo di 'klasse]
neighbor (masc.)	**vicino** (m)	[vi'ʧino]
neighbor (fem.)	**vicina** (f)	[vi'ʧina]
neighbors	**vicini** (m pl)	[vi'ʧini]

HUMAN BODY. MEDICINE

T&P Books Publishing

61. Head

head	**testa** (f)	['testa]
face	**viso** (m)	['vizo]
nose	**naso** (m)	['nazo]
mouth	**bocca** (f)	['bokka]
eye	**occhio** (m)	['okkio]
eyes	**occhi** (m pl)	['okki]
pupil	**pupilla** (f)	[pu'pilla]
eyebrow	**sopracciglio** (m)	[sopra'tʃiʎʎo]
eyelash	**ciglio** (m)	['tʃiʎʎo]
eyelid	**palpebra** (f)	['palpebra]
tongue	**lingua** (f)	['lingua]
tooth	**dente** (m)	['dente]
lips	**labbra** (f pl)	['labbra]
cheekbones	**zigomi** (m pl)	['dzigomi]
gum	**gengiva** (f)	[dʒen'dʒiva]
palate	**palato** (m)	[pa'lato]
nostrils	**narici** (f pl)	[na'ritʃi]
chin	**mento** (m)	['mento]
jaw	**mascella** (f)	[ma'ʃella]
cheek	**guancia** (f)	['gwantʃa]
forehead	**fronte** (f)	['fronte]
temple	**tempia** (f)	['tempia]
ear	**orecchio** (m)	[o'rekkio]
back of the head	**nuca** (f)	['nuka]
neck	**collo** (m)	['kollo]
throat	**gola** (f)	['gola]
hair	**capelli** (m pl)	[ka'pelli]
hairstyle	**pettinatura** (f)	[pettina'tura]
haircut	**taglio** (m)	['taʎʎo]
wig	**parrucca** (f)	['parrukka]
mustache	**baffi** (m pl)	['baffi]
beard	**barba** (f)	['barba]
to have (a beard, etc.)	**portare** (vt)	[por'tare]
braid	**treccia** (f)	['tretʃa]
sideburns	**basette** (f pl)	[ba'zette]
red-haired (adj)	**rosso**	['rosso]
gray (hair)	**brizzolato**	[brittso'lato]

bald (adj)	**calvo**	['kalvo]
bald patch	**calvizie** (f)	[kal'vitsie]
ponytail	**coda** (f) **di cavallo**	['koda di ka'vallo]
bangs	**frangetta** (f)	[fran'dʒetta]

62. Human body

hand	**mano** (f)	['mano]
arm	**braccio** (m)	['bratʃo]
finger	**dito** (m)	['dito]
toe	**dito** (m) **del piede**	['dito del 'pjede]
thumb	**pollice** (m)	['pollitʃe]
little finger	**mignolo** (m)	[mi'ɲolo]
nail	**unghia** (f)	['ungia]
fist	**pugno** (m)	['puɲo]
palm	**palmo** (m)	['palmo]
wrist	**polso** (m)	['polso]
forearm	**avambraccio** (m)	[avam'bratʃo]
elbow	**gomito** (m)	['gomito]
shoulder	**spalla** (f)	['spalla]
leg	**gamba** (f)	['gamba]
foot	**pianta** (f) **del piede**	['pjanta del 'pjede]
knee	**ginocchio** (m)	[dʒi'nokkio]
calf (part of leg)	**polpaccio** (m)	[pol'patʃo]
hip	**anca** (f)	['anka]
heel	**tallone** (m)	[tal'lone]
body	**corpo** (m)	['korpo]
stomach	**pancia** (f)	['pantʃa]
chest	**petto** (m)	['petto]
breast	**seno** (m)	['seno]
flank	**fianco** (m)	['fjanko]
back	**schiena** (f)	['skjena]
lower back	**zona** (f) **lombare**	['dzona lom'bare]
waist	**vita** (f)	['vita]
navel (belly button)	**ombelico** (m)	[ombe'liko]
buttocks	**natiche** (f pl)	['natike]
bottom	**sedere** (m)	[se'dere]
beauty mark	**neo** (m)	['neo]
birthmark (café au lait spot)	**voglia** (f)	['voʎʎa]
tattoo	**tatuaggio** (m)	[tatu'adʒo]
scar	**cicatrice** (f)	[tʃika'tritʃe]

63. Diseases

sickness	**malattia** (f)	[malat'tia]
to be sick	**essere malato**	['essere ma'lato]
health	**salute** (f)	[sa'lute]
runny nose (coryza)	**raffreddore** (m)	[raffred'dore]
tonsillitis	**tonsillite** (f)	[tonsil'lite]
cold (illness)	**raffreddore** (m)	[raffred'dore]
to catch a cold	**raffreddarsi** (vr)	[raffred'darsi]
bronchitis	**bronchite** (f)	[bron'kite]
pneumonia	**polmonite** (f)	[polmo'nite]
flu, influenza	**influenza** (f)	[influ'entsa]
nearsighted (adj)	**miope**	['miope]
farsighted (adj)	**presbite**	['prezbite]
strabismus (crossed eyes)	**strabismo** (m)	[stra'bizmo]
cross-eyed (adj)	**strabico**	['strabiko]
cataract	**cateratta** (f)	[kate'ratta]
glaucoma	**glaucoma** (m)	[glau'koma]
stroke	**ictus** (m) **cerebrale**	['iktus tʃere'brale]
heart attack	**attacco** (m) **di cuore**	[at'tako di ku'ore]
myocardial infarction	**infarto** (m) **miocardico**	[in'farto miokar'diko]
paralysis	**paralisi** (f)	[pa'ralizi]
to paralyze (vt)	**paralizzare** (vt)	[paralid'dzare]
allergy	**allergia** (f)	[aller'dʒia]
asthma	**asma** (f)	['azma]
diabetes	**diabete** (m)	[dia'bete]
toothache	**mal** (m) **di denti**	[mal di 'denti]
caries	**carie** (f)	['karie]
diarrhea	**diarrea** (f)	[diar'rea]
constipation	**stitichezza** (f)	[stiti'kettsa]
stomach upset	**disturbo** (m) **gastrico**	[di'sturbo 'gastriko]
food poisoning	**intossicazione** (f) **alimentare**	[intossika'tsjone alimen'tare]
to get food poisoning	**intossicarsi** (vr)	[intossi'karsi]
arthritis	**artrite** (f)	[ar'trite]
rickets	**rachitide** (f)	[ra'kitide]
rheumatism	**reumatismo** (m)	[reuma'tizmo]
atherosclerosis	**aterosclerosi** (f)	[ateroskle'rozi]
gastritis	**gastrite** (f)	[ga'strite]
appendicitis	**appendicite** (f)	[appendi'tʃite]
cholecystitis	**colecistite** (f)	[koletʃi'stite]
ulcer	**ulcera** (f)	['ultʃera]

measles	morbillo (m)	[mor'billo]
rubella (German measles)	rosolia (f)	[rozo'lia]
jaundice	itterizia (f)	[itte'ritsia]
hepatitis	epatite (f)	[epa'tite]

schizophrenia	schizofrenia (f)	[skidzofre'nia]
rabies (hydrophobia)	rabbia (f)	['rabbia]
neurosis	nevrosi (f)	[ne'vrozi]
concussion	commozione (f) cerebrale	[kommo'tsjone tʃere'brale]

cancer	cancro (m)	['kankro]
sclerosis	sclerosi (f)	[skle'rozi]
multiple sclerosis	sclerosi (f) multipla	[skle'rozi 'multipla]

alcoholism	alcolismo (m)	[alko'lizmo]
alcoholic (n)	alcolizzato (m)	[alkolid'dzato]
syphilis	sifilide (f)	[si'filide]
AIDS	AIDS (m)	['aids]

tumor	tumore (m)	[tu'more]
malignant (adj)	maligno	[ma'liɲo]
benign (adj)	benigno	[be'niɲo]
fever	febbre (f)	['febbre]
malaria	malaria (f)	[ma'laria]
gangrene	cancrena (f)	[kan'krena]
seasickness	mal (m) di mare	[mal di 'mare]
epilepsy	epilessia (f)	[epiles'sia]

epidemic	epidemia (f)	[epide'mia]
typhus	tifo (m)	['tifo]
tuberculosis	tubercolosi (f)	[tuberko'lozi]
cholera	colera (m)	[ko'lera]
plague (bubonic ~)	peste (f)	['peste]

64. Symptoms. Treatments. Part 1

symptom	sintomo (m)	['sintomo]
temperature	temperatura (f)	[tempera'tura]
high temperature (fever)	febbre (f) alta	['febbre 'alta]
pulse (heartbeat)	polso (m)	['polso]

dizziness (vertigo)	capogiro (m)	[kapo'dʒiro]
hot (adj)	caldo	['kaldo]
shivering	brivido (m)	['brivido]
pale (e.g., ~ face)	pallido	['pallido]

cough	tosse (f)	['tosse]
to cough (vi)	tossire (vi)	[tos'sire]
to sneeze (vi)	starnutire (vi)	[starnu'tire]
faint	svenimento (m)	[zveni'mento]

to faint (vi)	svenire (vi)	[zve'nire]
bruise (hématome)	livido (m)	['livido]
bump (lump)	bernoccolo (m)	[ber'nokkolo]
to bang (bump)	farsi un livido	['farsi un 'livido]
contusion (bruise)	contusione (f)	[kontu'zjone]
to get a bruise	farsi male	['farsi 'male]
to limp (vi)	zoppicare (vi)	[dzoppi'kare]
dislocation	slogatura (f)	[zloga'tura]
to dislocate (vt)	slogarsi (vr)	[zlo'garsi]
fracture	frattura (f)	[frat'tura]
to have a fracture	fratturarsi (vr)	[frattu'rarsi]
cut (e.g., paper ~)	taglio (m)	['taʎʎo]
to cut oneself	tagliarsi (vr)	[taʎ'ʎarsi]
bleeding	emorragia (f)	[emorra'dʒia]
burn (injury)	scottatura (f)	[skotta'tura]
to get burned	scottarsi (vr)	[skot'tarsi]
to prick (vt)	pungere (vt)	['pundʒere]
to prick oneself	pungersi (vr)	['pundʒersi]
to injure (vt)	ferire (vt)	[fe'rire]
injury	ferita (f)	[fe'rita]
wound	lesione (f)	[le'zjone]
trauma	trauma (m)	['trauma]
to be delirious	delirare (vi)	[deli'rare]
to stutter (vi)	tartagliare (vi)	[tartaʎ'ʎare]
sunstroke	colpo (m) di sole	['kolpo di 'sole]

65. Symptoms. Treatments. Part 2

pain, ache	dolore (m), male (m)	[do'lore], ['male]
splinter (in foot, etc.)	scheggia (f)	['skedʒa]
sweat (perspiration)	sudore (m)	[su'dore]
to sweat (perspire)	sudare (vi)	[su'dare]
vomiting	vomito (m)	['vomito]
convulsions	convulsioni (f pl)	[konvul'sjoni]
pregnant (adj)	incinta	[in'tʃinta]
to be born	nascere (vi)	['naʃere]
delivery, labor	parto (m)	['parto]
to deliver (~ a baby)	essere in travaglio	['essere in tra'vaʎʎo]
abortion	aborto (m)	[a'borto]
breathing, respiration	respirazione (f)	[respira'tsjone]
in-breath (inhalation)	inspirazione (f)	[inspira'tsjone]
out-breath (exhalation)	espirazione (f)	[espira'tsjone]

to exhale (breathe out)	espirare (vi)	[espi'rare]
to inhale (vi)	inspirare (vi)	[inspi'rare]
disabled person	invalido (m)	[in'valido]
cripple	storpio (m)	['storpjo]
drug addict	battaglia (f)	[bat'taʎʎa]
deaf (adj)	sordo	['sordo]
mute (adj)	muto	['muto]
deaf mute (adj)	sordomuto	[sordo'muto]
mad, insane (adj)	matto	['matto]
madman (demented person)	matto (m)	['matto]
madwoman	matta (f)	['matta]
to go insane	impazzire (vi)	[impat'tsire]
gene	gene (m)	['dʒene]
immunity	immunità (f)	[immuni'ta]
hereditary (adj)	ereditario	[eredi'tario]
congenital (adj)	innato	[in'nato]
virus	virus (m)	['virus]
microbe	microbo (m)	['mikrobo]
bacterium	batterio (m)	[bat'terio]
infection	infezione (f)	[infe'tsjone]

66. Symptoms. Treatments. Part 3

hospital	ospedale (m)	[ospe'dale]
patient	paziente (m)	[pa'tsjente]
diagnosis	diagnosi (f)	[di'aɲozi]
cure	cura (f)	['kura]
medical treatment	trattamento (m)	[tratta'mento]
to get treatment	curarsi (vr)	[ku'rarsi]
to treat (~ a patient)	curare (vt)	[ku'rare]
to nurse (look after)	accudire	[akku'dire]
care (nursing ~)	assistenza (f)	[assi'stentsa]
operation, surgery	operazione (f)	[opera'tsjone]
to bandage (head, limb)	bendare (vt)	[ben'dare]
bandaging	fasciatura (f)	[faʃa'tura]
vaccination	vaccinazione (f)	[vatʃina'tsjone]
to vaccinate (vt)	vaccinare (vt)	[vatʃi'nare]
injection, shot	iniezione (f)	[inje'tsjone]
to give an injection	fare una puntura	['fare 'una pun'tura]
attack	attacco (m)	[at'takko]
amputation	amputazione (f)	[amputa'tsjone]

to amputate (vt)	amputare (vt)	[ampu'tare]
coma	coma (m)	['koma]
to be in a coma	essere in coma	['essere in 'koma]
intensive care	rianimazione (f)	[rianima'tsjone]

to recover (~ from flu)	guarire (vi)	[gwa'rire]
condition (patient's ~)	stato (f)	['stato]
consciousness	conoscenza (f)	[kono'ʃentsa]
memory (faculty)	memoria (f)	[me'moria]

to pull out (tooth)	estrarre (vt)	[e'strarre]
filling	otturazione (f)	[ottura'tsjone]
to fill (a tooth)	otturare (vt)	[ottu'rare]

| hypnosis | ipnosi (f) | [ip'nozi] |
| to hypnotize (vt) | ipnotizzare (vt) | [ipnotid'dzare] |

67. Medicine. Drugs. Accessories

medicine, drug	medicina (f)	[medi'tʃina]
remedy	rimedio (m)	[ri'medio]
to prescribe (vt)	prescrivere (vt)	[pres'krivere]
prescription	prescrizione (f)	[preskri'tsjone]

tablet, pill	compressa (f)	[kom'pressa]
ointment	unguento (m)	[un'gwento]
ampule	fiala (f)	[fi'ala]
mixture, solution	pozione (f)	[po'tsjone]
syrup	sciroppo (m)	[ʃi'roppo]
capsule	pillola (f)	['pillola]
powder	polverina (f)	[polve'rina]

gauze bandage	benda (f)	['benda]
cotton wool	ovatta (f)	[o'vatta]
iodine	iodio (m)	[i'odio]

| Band-Aid | cerotto (m) | [tʃe'rotto] |
| eyedropper | contagocce (m) | [konta'gotʃe] |

| thermometer | termometro (m) | [ter'mometro] |
| syringe | siringa (f) | [si'ringa] |

| wheelchair | sedia (f) a rotelle | ['sedia a ro'telle] |
| crutches | stampelle (f pl) | [stam'pelle] |

painkiller	analgesico (m)	[anal'dʒeziko]
laxative	lassativo (m)	[lassa'tivo]
spirits (ethanol)	alcol (m)	[al'kol]
medicinal herbs	erba (f) officinale	['erba offitʃi'nale]
herbal (~ tea)	d'erbe	['derbe]

APARTMENT

T&P Books Publishing

68. Apartment

apartment	**appartamento** (m)	[apparta'mento]
room	**camera** (f), **stanza** (f)	['kamera], ['stantsa]
bedroom	**camera** (f) **da letto**	['kamera da 'letto]
dining room	**sala** (f) **da pranzo**	['sala da 'prantso]
living room	**salotto** (m)	[sa'lotto]
study (home office)	**studio** (m)	['studio]
entry room	**ingresso** (m)	[in'gresso]
bathroom (room with a bath or shower)	**bagno** (m)	['baɲo]
half bath	**gabinetto** (m)	[gabi'netto]
ceiling	**soffitto** (m)	[sof'fitto]
floor	**pavimento** (m)	[pavi'mento]
corner	**angolo** (m)	['angolo]

69. Furniture. Interior

furniture	**mobili** (m pl)	['mobili]
table	**tavolo** (m)	['tavolo]
chair	**sedia** (f)	['sedia]
bed	**letto** (m)	['letto]
couch, sofa	**divano** (m)	[di'vano]
armchair	**poltrona** (f)	[pol'trona]
bookcase	**libreria** (f)	[libre'ria]
shelf	**ripiano** (m)	[ri'pjano]
wardrobe	**armadio** (m)	[ar'madio]
coat rack (wall-mounted ~)	**attaccapanni** (m) **da parete**	[attakka'panni da pa'rete]
coat stand	**appendiabiti** (m) **da terra**	[apen'djabiti da terra]
bureau, dresser	**comò** (m)	[ko'mo]
coffee table	**tavolino** (m) **da salotto**	[tavo'lina da sa'lotto]
mirror	**specchio** (m)	['spekkio]
carpet	**tappeto** (m)	[tap'peto]
rug, small carpet	**tappetino** (m)	[tappe'tino]
fireplace	**camino** (m)	[ka'mino]
candle	**candela** (f)	[kan'dela]

candlestick	**candeliere** (m)	[kande'ljere]
drapes	**tende** (f pl)	['tende]
wallpaper	**carta** (f) **da parati**	['karta da pa'rati]
blinds (jalousie)	**tende** (f pl) **alla veneziana**	['tende alla vene'tsjana]
table lamp	**lampada** (f) **da tavolo**	['lampada da 'tavolo]
wall lamp (sconce)	**lampada** (f) **da parete**	['lampada da pa'rete]
floor lamp	**lampada** (f) **a stelo**	['lampada a 'stelo]
chandelier	**lampadario** (m)	[lampa'dario]
leg (of chair, table)	**gamba** (f)	['gamba]
armrest	**bracciolo** (m)	['bratʃolo]
back (backrest)	**spalliera** (f)	[spal'ljera]
drawer	**cassetto** (m)	[kas'setto]

70. Bedding

bedclothes	**biancheria** (f) **da letto**	[bjanke'ria da 'letto]
pillow	**cuscino** (m)	[ku'ʃino]
pillowcase	**federa** (f)	['federa]
duvet, comforter	**coperta** (f)	[ko'perta]
sheet	**lenzuolo** (m)	[lentsu'olo]
bedspread	**copriletto** (m)	[kopri'letto]

71. Kitchen

kitchen	**cucina** (f)	[ku'tʃina]
gas	**gas** (m)	[gas]
gas stove (range)	**fornello** (m) **a gas**	[for'nello a gas]
electric stove	**fornello** (m) **elettrico**	[for'nello e'lettriko]
oven	**forno** (m)	['forno]
microwave oven	**forno** (m) **a microonde**	['forno a mikro'onde]
refrigerator	**frigorifero** (m)	[frigo'rifero]
freezer	**congelatore** (m)	[kondʒela'tore]
dishwasher	**lavastoviglie** (f)	[lavasto'viʎʎe]
meat grinder	**tritacarne** (m)	[trita'karne]
juicer	**spremifrutta** (m)	[spremi'frutta]
toaster	**tostapane** (m)	[tosta'pane]
mixer	**mixer** (m)	['mikser]
coffee machine	**macchina** (f) **da caffè**	['makkina da kaf'fe]
coffee pot	**caffettiera** (f)	[kaffet'tjera]
coffee grinder	**macinacaffè** (m)	[matʃinakaf'fe]
kettle	**bollitore** (m)	[bolli'tore]
teapot	**teiera** (f)	[te'jera]

lid	**coperchio** (m)	[ko'perkio]
tea strainer	**colino** (m) **da tè**	[ko'lino da te]
spoon	**cucchiaio** (m)	[kuk'kjajo]
teaspoon	**cucchiaino** (m) **da tè**	[kuk'kjajno da 'te]
soup spoon	**cucchiaio** (m)	[kuk'kjajo]
fork	**forchetta** (f)	[for'ketta]
knife	**coltello** (m)	[kol'tello]
tableware (dishes)	**stoviglie** (f pl)	[sto'viʎʎe]
plate (dinner ~)	**piatto** (m)	['pjatto]
saucer	**piattino** (m)	[pjat'tino]
shot glass	**cicchetto** (m)	[tʃik'ketto]
glass (tumbler)	**bicchiere** (m)	[bik'kjere]
cup	**tazzina** (f)	[tat'tsina]
sugar bowl	**zuccheriera** (f)	[dzukke'rjera]
salt shaker	**saliera** (f)	[sa'ljera]
pepper shaker	**pepiera** (f)	[pe'pjera]
butter dish	**burriera** (f)	[bur'rjera]
stock pot (soup pot)	**pentola** (f)	['pentola]
frying pan (skillet)	**padella** (f)	[pa'della]
ladle	**mestolo** (m)	['mestolo]
colander	**colapasta** (m)	[kola'pasta]
tray (serving ~)	**vassoio** (m)	[vas'sojo]
bottle	**bottiglia** (f)	[bot'tiʎʎa]
jar (glass)	**barattolo** (m) **di vetro**	[ba'rattolo di 'vetro]
can	**latta** (f), **lattina** (f)	['latta], [lat'tina]
bottle opener	**apribottiglie** (m)	[apribot'tiʎʎe]
can opener	**apriscatole** (m)	[apri'skatole]
corkscrew	**cavatappi** (m)	[kava'tappi]
filter	**filtro** (m)	['filtro]
to filter (vt)	**filtrare** (vt)	[fil'trare]
trash, garbage (food waste, etc.)	**spazzatura** (f)	[spattsa'tura]
trash can (kitchen ~)	**pattumiera** (f)	[pattu'mjera]

72. Bathroom

bathroom	**bagno** (m)	['baɲo]
water	**acqua** (f)	['akwa]
faucet	**rubinetto** (m)	[rubi'netto]
hot water	**acqua** (f) **calda**	['akwa 'kalda]
cold water	**acqua** (f) **fredda**	['akwa 'fredda]
toothpaste	**dentifricio** (m)	[denti'fritʃo]

| to brush one's teeth | lavarsi i denti | [la'varsi i 'denti] |
| toothbrush | spazzolino (m) da denti | [spatso'lino da 'denti] |

to shave (vi)	rasarsi (vr)	[ra'zarsi]
shaving foam	schiuma (f) da barba	['skjuma da 'barba]
razor	rasoio (m)	[ra'zojo]

to wash (one's hands, etc.)	lavare (vt)	[la'vare]
to take a bath	fare un bagno	['fare un 'baɲo]
shower	doccia (f)	['dotʃa]
to take a shower	fare una doccia	['fare 'una 'dotʃa]

bathtub	vasca (f) da bagno	['vaska da 'baɲo]
toilet (toilet bowl)	water (m)	['vater]
sink (washbasin)	lavandino (m)	[lavan'dino]

| soap | sapone (m) | [sa'pone] |
| soap dish | porta (m) sapone | ['porta sa'pone] |

sponge	spugna (f)	['spuɲa]
shampoo	shampoo (m)	['ʃampo]
towel	asciugamano (m)	[aʃuga'mano]
bathrobe	accappatoio (m)	[akkappa'tojo]

laundry (laundering)	bucato (m)	[bu'kato]
washing machine	lavatrice (f)	[lava'tritʃe]
to do the laundry	fare il bucato	['fare il bu'kato]
laundry detergent	detersivo (m) per il bucato	[deter'sivo per il bu'kato]

73. Household appliances

TV set	televisore (m)	[televi'zore]
tape recorder	registratore (m) a nastro	[redʒistra'tore a 'nastro]
VCR (video recorder)	videoregistratore (m)	[video·redʒistra'tore]
radio	radio (f)	['radio]
player (CD, MP3, etc.)	lettore (m)	[let'tore]

video projector	videoproiettore (m)	[video·projet'tore]
home movie theater	home cinema (m)	['om 'tʃinema]
DVD player	lettore (m) DVD	[let'tore divu'di]
amplifier	amplificatore (m)	[amplifika'tore]
video game console	console (f) video giochi	['konsole 'video 'dʒoki]

video camera	videocamera (f)	[video·'kamera]
camera (photo)	macchina (f) fotografica	['makkina foto'grafika]
digital camera	fotocamera (f) digitale	[foto'kamera didʒi'tale]

| vacuum cleaner | aspirapolvere (m) | [aspira·'polvere] |
| iron (e.g., steam ~) | ferro (m) da stiro | ['ferro da 'stiro] |

ironing board	asse (f) da stiro	['asse da 'stiro]
telephone	telefono (m)	[te'lefono]
cell phone	telefonino (m)	[telefo'nino]
typewriter	macchina (f) da scrivere	['makkina da 'skrivere]
sewing machine	macchina (f) da cucire	['makkina da ku'tʃire]
microphone	microfono (m)	[mi'krofono]
headphones	cuffia (f)	['kuffia]
remote control (TV)	telecomando (m)	[teleko'mando]
CD, compact disc	CD (m)	[tʃi'di]
cassette, tape	cassetta (f)	[kas'setta]
vinyl record	disco (m)	['disko]

THE EARTH. WEATHER

T&P Books Publishing

space	cosmo (m)	['kozmo]
space (as adj)	cosmico, spaziale	['kozmiko], [spa'tsjale]
outer space	spazio (m) cosmico	['spatsio 'kozmiko]
world	mondo (m)	['mondo]
universe	universo (m)	[uni'verso]
galaxy	galassia (f)	[ga'lassia]
star	stella (f)	['stella]
constellation	costellazione (f)	[kostella'tsjone]
planet	pianeta (m)	[pja'neta]
satellite	satellite (m)	[sa'tellite]
meteorite	meteorite (m)	[meteo'rite]
comet	cometa (f)	[ko'meta]
asteroid	asteroide (m)	[aste'roide]
orbit	orbita (f)	['orbita]
to revolve	ruotare (vi)	[ruo'tare]
(~ around the Earth)		
atmosphere	atmosfera (f)	[atmo'sfera]
the Sun	il Sole	[il 'sole]
solar system	sistema (m) solare	[si'stema so'lare]
solar eclipse	eclisse (f) solare	[e'klisse so'lare]
the Earth	la Terra	[la 'terra]
the Moon	la Luna	[la 'luna]
Mars	Marte (m)	['marte]
Venus	Venere (f)	['venere]
Jupiter	Giove (m)	['dʒove]
Saturn	Saturno (m)	[sa'turno]
Mercury	Mercurio (m)	[mer'kurio]
Uranus	Urano (m)	[u'rano]
Neptune	Nettuno (m)	[net'tuno]
Pluto	Plutone (m)	[plu'tone]
Milky Way	Via (f) Lattea	['via 'lattea]
Great Bear (Ursa Major)	Orsa (f) Maggiore	['orsa ma'dʒore]
North Star	Stella (f) Polare	['stella po'lare]
Martian	marziano (m)	[mar'tsjano]
extraterrestrial (n)	extraterrestre (m)	[ekstrater'restre]

| alien | alieno (m) | [a'ljeno] |
| flying saucer | disco (m) volante | ['disko vo'lante] |

spaceship	nave (f) spaziale	['nave spa'tsjale]
space station	stazione (f) spaziale	[sta'tsjone spa'tsjale]
blast-off	lancio (m)	['lantʃo]

engine	motore (m)	[mo'tore]
nozzle	ugello (m)	[u'dʒello]
fuel	combustibile (m)	[kombu'stibile]

cockpit, flight deck	cabina (f) di pilotaggio	[ka'bina di pilo'tadʒio]
antenna	antenna (f)	[an'tenna]
porthole	oblò (m)	[ob'lo]
solar panel	batteria (f) solare	[batte'ria so'lare]
spacesuit	scafandro (m)	[ska'fandro]

| weightlessness | imponderabilità (f) | [imponderabili'ta] |
| oxygen | ossigeno (m) | [os'sidʒeno] |

| docking (in space) | aggancio (m) | [ag'gantʃo] |
| to dock (vi, vt) | agganciarsi (vr) | [aggan'tʃarsi] |

observatory	osservatorio (m)	[osserva'torio]
telescope	telescopio (m)	[tele'skopio]
to observe (vt)	osservare (vt)	[osser'vare]
to explore (vt)	esplorare (vt)	[esplo'rare]

75. The Earth

the Earth	la Terra	[la 'terra]
the globe (the Earth)	globo (m) terrestre	['globo ter'restre]
planet	pianeta (m)	[pja'neta]

atmosphere	atmosfera (f)	[atmo'sfera]
geography	geografia (f)	[dʒeogra'fia]
nature	natura (f)	[na'tura]

globe (table ~)	mappamondo (m)	[mappa'mondo]
map	carta (f) geografica	['karta dʒeo'grafika]
atlas	atlante (m)	[a'tlante]

Europe	Europa (f)	[eu'ropa]
Asia	Asia (f)	['azia]
Africa	Africa (f)	['afrika]
Australia	Australia (f)	[au'stralia]

America	America (f)	[a'merika]
North America	America (f) del Nord	[a'merika del nord]
South America	America (f) del Sud	[a'merika del sud]

| Antarctica | **Antartide** (f) | [an'tartide] |
| the Arctic | **Artico** (m) | ['artiko] |

76. Cardinal directions

north	**nord** (m)	[nord]
to the north	**a nord**	[a nord]
in the north	**al nord**	[al nord]
northern (adj)	**del nord**	[del nord]

south	**sud** (m)	[sud]
to the south	**a sud**	[a sud]
in the south	**al sud**	[al sud]
southern (adj)	**del sud**	[del sud]

west	**ovest** (m)	['ovest]
to the west	**a ovest**	[a 'ovest]
in the west	**all'ovest**	[all 'ovest]
western (adj)	**dell'ovest, occidentale**	[dell 'ovest], [otʃiden'tale]

east	**est** (m)	[est]
to the east	**a est**	[a est]
in the east	**all'est**	[all 'est]
eastern (adj)	**dell'est, orientale**	[dell 'est], [orien'tale]

77. Sea. Ocean

sea	**mare** (m)	['mare]
ocean	**oceano** (m)	[o'tʃeano]
gulf (bay)	**golfo** (m)	['golfo]
straits	**stretto** (m)	['stretto]

land (solid ground)	**terra** (f)	['terra]
continent (mainland)	**continente** (m)	[konti'nente]
island	**isola** (f)	['izola]
peninsula	**penisola** (f)	[pe'nizola]
archipelago	**arcipelago** (m)	[artʃi'pelago]

bay, cove	**baia** (f)	['baja]
harbor	**porto** (m)	['porto]
lagoon	**laguna** (f)	[la'guna]
cape	**capo** (m)	['kapo]

atoll	**atollo** (m)	[a'tollo]
reef	**scogliera** (f)	[skoʎ'ʎera]
coral	**corallo** (m)	[ko'rallo]
coral reef	**barriera** (f) **corallina**	[bar'rjera koral'lina]
deep (adj)	**profondo**	[pro'fondo]

depth (deep water)	**profondità** (f)	[profondi'ta]
abyss	**abisso** (m)	[a'bisso]
trench (e.g., Mariana ~)	**fossa** (f)	['fossa]
current (Ocean ~)	**corrente** (f)	[kor'rente]
to surround (bathe)	**circondare** (vt)	[tʃirkon'dare]
shore	**litorale** (m)	[lito'rale]
coast	**costa** (f)	['kosta]
flow (flood tide)	**alta marea** (f)	['alta ma'rea]
ebb (ebb tide)	**bassa marea** (f)	['bassa ma'rea]
shoal	**banco** (m) **di sabbia**	['banko di 'sabbia]
bottom (~ of the sea)	**fondo** (m)	['fondo]
wave	**onda** (f)	['onda]
crest (~ of a wave)	**cresta** (f) **dell'onda**	['kresta dell 'onda]
spume (sea foam)	**schiuma** (f)	['skjuma]
storm (sea storm)	**tempesta** (f)	[tem'pesta]
hurricane	**uragano** (m)	[ura'gano]
tsunami	**tsunami** (m)	[tsu'nami]
calm (dead ~)	**bonaccia** (f)	[bo'natʃa]
quiet, calm (adj)	**tranquillo**	[tran'kwillo]
pole	**polo** (m)	['polo]
polar (adj)	**polare**	[po'lare]
latitude	**latitudine** (f)	[lati'tudine]
longitude	**longitudine** (f)	[londʒi'tudine]
parallel	**parallelo** (m)	[paral'lelo]
equator	**equatore** (m)	[ekwa'tore]
sky	**cielo** (m)	['tʃelo]
horizon	**orizzonte** (m)	[orid'dzonte]
air	**aria** (f)	['aria]
lighthouse	**faro** (m)	['faro]
to dive (vi)	**tuffarsi** (vr)	[tuf'farsi]
to sink (ab. boat)	**affondare** (vi)	[affon'dare]
treasures	**tesori** (m)	[te'zori]

78. Seas' and Oceans' names

Atlantic Ocean	**Oceano** (m) **Atlantico**	[o'tʃeano at'lantiko]
Indian Ocean	**Oceano** (m) **Indiano**	[o'tʃeano indi'ano]
Pacific Ocean	**Oceano** (m) **Pacifico**	[o'tʃeano pa'tʃifiko]
Arctic Ocean	**mar** (m) **Glaciale Artico**	[mar gla'tʃale 'artiko]
Black Sea	**mar** (m) **Nero**	[mar 'nero]
Red Sea	**mar** (m) **Rosso**	[mar 'rosso]

| Yellow Sea | mar (m) Giallo | [mar 'dʒallo] |
| White Sea | mar (m) Bianco | [mar 'bjanko] |

Caspian Sea	mar (m) Caspio	[mar 'kaspio]
Dead Sea	mar (m) Morto	[mar 'morto]
Mediterranean Sea	mar (m) Mediterraneo	[mar mediter'raneo]

| Aegean Sea | mar (m) Egeo | [mar e'dʒeo] |
| Adriatic Sea | mar (m) Adriatico | [mar adri'atiko] |

Arabian Sea	mar (m) Arabico	[mar a'rabiko]
Sea of Japan	mar (m) del Giappone	[mar del dʒap'pone]
Bering Sea	mare (m) di Bering	['mare di 'bering]
South China Sea	mar (m) Cinese meridionale	[mar t͡ʃi'neze meridio'nale]

Coral Sea	mar (m) dei Coralli	[mar 'dei ko'ralli]
Tasman Sea	mar (m) di Tasmania	[mar di taz'mania]
Caribbean Sea	mar (m) dei Caraibi	[mar dei kara'ibi]

| Barents Sea | mare (m) di Barents | ['mare di 'barents] |
| Kara Sea | mare (m) di Kara | ['mare di 'kara] |

North Sea	mare (m) del Nord	['mare del nord]
Baltic Sea	mar (m) Baltico	[mar 'baltiko]
Norwegian Sea	mare (m) di Norvegia	['mare di nor'vedʒa]

79. Mountains

mountain	monte (m), montagna (f)	['monte], [mon'taɲa]
mountain range	catena (f) montuosa	[ka'tena montu'oza]
mountain ridge	crinale (m)	[kri'nale]

summit, top	cima (f)	['t͡ʃima]
peak	picco (m)	['pikko]
foot (~ of the mountain)	piedi (m pl)	['pjede]
slope (mountainside)	pendio (m)	[pen'dio]

volcano	vulcano (m)	[vul'kano]
active volcano	vulcano (m) attivo	[vul'kano at'tivo]
dormant volcano	vulcano (m) inattivo	[vul'kano inat'tivo]

eruption	eruzione (f)	[eru'tsjone]
crater	cratere (m)	[kra'tere]
magma	magma (m)	['magma]
lava	lava (f)	['lava]
molten (~ lava)	fuso	['fuzo]

| canyon | canyon (m) | ['kenjon] |
| gorge | gola (f) | ['gola] |

| crevice | crepaccio (m) | [kre'patʃo] |
| abyss (chasm) | precipizio (m) | [pretʃi'pitsio] |

pass, col	passo (m), valico (m)	['passo], ['valiko]
plateau	altopiano (m)	[alto'pjano]
cliff	falesia (f)	[fa'lezia]
hill	collina (f)	[kol'lina]

glacier	ghiacciaio (m)	[gja'tʃajo]
waterfall	cascata (f)	[kas'kata]
geyser	geyser (m)	['gejzer]
lake	lago (m)	['lago]

plain	pianura (f)	[pja'nura]
landscape	paesaggio (m)	[pae'zadʒo]
echo	eco (f)	['eko]

alpinist	alpinista (m)	[alpi'nista]
rock climber	scalatore (m)	[skala'tore]
to conquer (in climbing)	conquistare (vt)	[konkwi'stare]
climb (an easy ~)	scalata (f)	[ska'lata]

80. Mountains names

The Alps	Alpi (f pl)	['alpi]
Mont Blanc	Monte (m) Bianco	['monte 'bjanko]
The Pyrenees	Pirenei (m pl)	[pire'nei]

The Carpathians	Carpazi (m pl)	[kar'patsi]
The Ural Mountains	gli Urali (m pl)	[ʎi u'rali]
The Caucasus Mountains	Caucaso (m)	['kaukazo]
Mount Elbrus	Monte (m) Elbrus	['monte 'elbrus]

The Altai Mountains	Monti (m pl) Altai	['monti al'taj]
The Tian Shan	Tien Shan (m)	[tjen 'ʃan]
The Pamir Mountains	Pamir (m)	[pa'mir]
The Himalayas	Himalaia (m)	[ima'laja]
Mount Everest	Everest (m)	['everest]

| The Andes | Ande (f pl) | ['ande] |
| Mount Kilimanjaro | Kilimangiaro (m) | [kiliman'dʒaro] |

81. Rivers

river	fiume (m)	['fjume]
spring (natural source)	fonte (f)	['fonte]
riverbed (river channel)	letto (m)	['letto]
basin (river valley)	bacino (m)	[ba'tʃino]

to flow into ...	sfociare nel ...	[sfo'tʃare nel]
tributary	affluente (m)	[afflu'ente]
bank (of river)	riva (f)	['riva]

current (stream)	corrente (f)	[kor'rente]
downstream (adv)	a valle	[a 'valle]
upstream (adv)	a monte	[a 'monte]

inundation	inondazione (f)	[inonda'tsjone]
flooding	piena (f)	['pjena]
to overflow (vi)	straripare (vi)	[strari'pare]
to flood (vt)	inondare (vt)	[inon'dare]

| shallow (shoal) | secca (f) | ['sekka] |
| rapids | rapida (f) | ['rapida] |

dam	diga (f)	['diga]
canal	canale (m)	[ka'nale]
reservoir (artificial lake)	bacino (m) di riserva	[ba'tʃino di ri'zerva]
sluice, lock	chiusa (f)	['kjuza]

water body (pond, etc.)	bacino (m) idrico	[ba'tʃino 'idriko]
swamp (marshland)	palude (f)	[pa'lude]
bog, marsh	pantano (m)	[pan'tano]
whirlpool	vortice (m)	['vortitʃe]

stream (brook)	ruscello (m)	[ru'ʃello]
drinking (ab. water)	potabile	[po'tabile]
fresh (~ water)	dolce	['doltʃe]

| ice | ghiaccio (m) | ['gjatʃo] |
| to freeze over (ab. river, etc.) | ghiacciarsi (vr) | [gja'tʃarsi] |

82. Rivers' names

| Seine | Senna (f) | ['senna] |
| Loire | Loira (f) | ['loira] |

Thames	Tamigi (m)	[ta'midʒi]
Rhine	Reno (m)	['reno]
Danube	Danubio (m)	[da'nubio]

Volga	Volga (m)	['volga]
Don	Don (m)	[don]
Lena	Lena (f)	['lena]

Yellow River	Fiume (m) Giallo	['fjume 'dʒallo]
Yangtze	Fiume (m) Azzurro	['fjume ad'dzurro]
Mekong	Mekong (m)	[me'kong]

Ganges	Gange (m)	['gandʒe]
Nile River	Nilo (m)	['nilo]
Congo River	Congo (m)	['kongo]
Okavango River	Okavango	[oka'vango]
Zambezi River	Zambesi (m)	[dzam'bezi]
Limpopo River	Limpopo (m)	['limpopo]
Mississippi River	Mississippi (m)	[missis'sippi]

83. Forest

| forest, wood | foresta (f) | [fo'resta] |
| forest (as adj) | forestale | [fores'tale] |

thick forest	foresta (f) fitta	[fo'resta 'fitta]
grove	boschetto (m)	[bos'ketto]
forest clearing	radura (f)	[ra'dura]

| thicket | roveto (m) | [ro'veto] |
| scrubland | boscaglia (f) | [bos'kaʎʎa] |

| footpath (troddenpath) | sentiero (m) | [sen'tjero] |
| gully | calanco (m) | [ka'lanko] |

tree	albero (m)	['albero]
leaf	foglia (f)	['foʎʎa]
leaves (foliage)	fogliame (m)	[foʎ'ʎame]

fall of leaves	caduta (f) delle foglie	[ka'duta 'delle 'foʎʎe]
to fall (ab. leaves)	cadere (vi)	[ka'dere]
top (of the tree)	cima (f)	['tʃima]

branch	ramo (m), ramoscello (m)	['ramo], [ramo'ʃello]
bough	ramo (m)	['ramo]
bud (on shrub, tree)	gemma (f)	['dʒemma]
needle (of pine tree)	ago (m)	['ago]
pine cone	pigna (f)	['piɲa]

tree hollow	cavità (f)	[kavi'ta]
nest	nido (m)	['nido]
burrow (animal hole)	tana (f)	['tana]

trunk	tronco (m)	['tronko]
root	radice (f)	[ra'ditʃe]
bark	corteccia (f)	[kor'tetʃa]
moss	musco (m)	['musko]

to uproot (remove trees or tree stumps)	sradicare (vt)	[zradi'kare]
to chop down	abbattere (vt)	[ab'battere]
to deforest (vt)	disboscare (vt)	[dizbo'skare]

tree stump	ceppo (m)	['ʧeppo]
campfire	falò (m)	[fa'lo]
forest fire	incendio (m) boschivo	[in'ʧendio bos'kivo]
to extinguish (vt)	spegnere (vt)	['speɲere]

forest ranger	guardia (f) forestale	['gwardia fores'tale]
protection	protezione (f)	[prote'tsjone]
to protect (~ nature)	proteggere (vt)	[pro'tedʒere]
poacher	bracconiere (m)	[brakko'njere]
steel trap	tagliola (f)	[taʎ'ʎoʎa]

| to gather, to pick (vt) | raccogliere (vt) | [rak'koʎʎere] |
| to lose one's way | perdersi (vr) | ['perdersi] |

84. Natural resources

natural resources	risorse (f pl) naturali	[ri'sorse natu'rali]
minerals	minerali (m pl)	[mine'rali]
deposits	deposito (m)	[de'pozito]
field (e.g., oilfield)	giacimento (m)	[dʒatʃi'mento]

to mine (extract)	estrarre (vt)	[e'strarre]
mining (extraction)	estrazione (f)	[estra'tsjone]
ore	minerale (m) grezzo	[mine'rale 'greddzo]
mine (e.g., for coal)	miniera (f)	[mi'njera]
shaft (mine ~)	pozzo (m) di miniera	['pottso di mi'njera]
miner	minatore (m)	[mina'tore]

| gas (natural ~) | gas (m) | [gas] |
| gas pipeline | gasdotto (m) | [gas'dotto] |

oil (petroleum)	petrolio (m)	[pe'trolio]
oil pipeline	oleodotto (m)	[oleo'dotto]
oil well	torre (f) di estrazione	['torre di estra'tsjone]
derrick (tower)	torre (f) di trivellazione	['torre di trivella'tsjone]
tanker	petroliera (f)	[petro'ljera]

sand	sabbia (f)	['sabbia]
limestone	calcare (m)	[kal'kare]
gravel	ghiaia (f)	['gjaja]
peat	torba (f)	['torba]
clay	argilla (f)	[ar'dʒilla]
coal	carbone (m)	[kar'bone]

iron (ore)	ferro (m)	['ferro]
gold	oro (m)	['oro]
silver	argento (m)	[ar'dʒento]
nickel	nichel (m)	['nikel]
copper	rame (m)	['rame]
zinc	zinco (m)	['dzinko]

manganese	**manganese** (m)	[manga'neze]
mercury	**mercurio** (m)	[mer'kurio]
lead	**piombo** (m)	['pjombo]
mineral	**minerale** (m)	[mine'rale]
crystal	**cristallo** (m)	[kris'tallo]
marble	**marmo** (m)	['marmo]
uranium	**uranio** (m)	[u'ranio]

85. Weather

weather	**tempo** (m)	['tempo]
weather forecast	**previsione** (f) **del tempo**	[previ'zjone del 'tempo]
temperature	**temperatura** (f)	[tempera'tura]
thermometer	**termometro** (m)	[ter'mometro]
barometer	**barometro** (m)	[ba'rometro]
humid (adj)	**umido**	['umido]
humidity	**umidità** (f)	[umidi'ta]
heat (extreme ~)	**caldo** (m), **afa** (f)	['kaldo], ['afa]
hot (torrid)	**molto caldo**	['molto 'kaldo]
it's hot	**fa molto caldo**	[fa 'molto 'kaldo]
it's warm	**fa caldo**	[fa 'kaldo]
warm (moderately hot)	**caldo**	['kaldo]
it's cold	**fa freddo**	[fa 'freddo]
cold (adj)	**freddo**	['freddo]
sun	**sole** (m)	['sole]
to shine (vi)	**splendere** (vi)	['splendere]
sunny (day)	**di sole**	[di 'sole]
to come up (vi)	**levarsi** (vr)	[le'varsi]
to set (vi)	**tramontare** (vi)	[tramon'tare]
cloud	**nuvola** (f)	['nuvola]
cloudy (adj)	**nuvoloso**	[nuvo'lozo]
rain cloud	**nube** (f) **di pioggia**	['nube di 'pjodʒa]
somber (gloomy)	**nuvoloso**	[nuvo'lozo]
rain	**pioggia** (f)	['pjodʒa]
it's raining	**piove**	['pjove]
rainy (~ day, weather)	**piovoso**	[pjo'vozo]
to drizzle (vi)	**piovigginare** (vi)	[pjovidʒi'nare]
pouring rain	**pioggia** (f) **torrenziale**	['pjodʒa torren'tsjale]
downpour	**acquazzone** (m)	[akwat'tsone]
heavy (e.g., ~ rain)	**forte**	['forte]
puddle	**pozzanghera** (f)	[pot'tsangera]
to get wet (in rain)	**bagnarsi** (vr)	[ba'ɲarsi]

fog (mist)	foschia (f), nebbia (f)	[fos'kia], ['nebbia]
foggy	nebbioso	[neb'bjozo]
snow	neve (f)	['neve]
it's snowing	nevica	['nevika]

86. Severe weather. Natural disasters

thunderstorm	temporale (m)	[tempo'rale]
lightning (~ strike)	fulmine (f)	['fulmine]
to flash (vi)	lampeggiare (vi)	[lampe'dʒare]

thunder	tuono (m)	[tu'ono]
to thunder (vi)	tuonare (vi)	[tuo'nare]
it's thundering	tuona	[tu'ona]

| hail | grandine (f) | ['grandine] |
| it's hailing | grandina | ['grandina] |

| to flood (vt) | inondare (vt) | [inon'dare] |
| flood, inundation | inondazione (f) | [inonda'tsjone] |

earthquake	terremoto (m)	[terre'moto]
tremor, shoke	scossa (f)	['skossa]
epicenter	epicentro (m)	[epi'tʃentro]

| eruption | eruzione (f) | [eru'tsjone] |
| lava | lava (f) | ['lava] |

twister	tromba (f) d'aria	['tromba 'daria]
tornado	tornado (m)	[tor'nado]
typhoon	tifone (m)	[ti'fone]

hurricane	uragano (m)	[ura'gano]
storm	tempesta (f)	[tem'pesta]
tsunami	tsunami (m)	[tsu'nami]

cyclone	ciclone (m)	[tʃi'klone]
bad weather	maltempo (m)	[mal'tempo]
fire (accident)	incendio (m)	[in'tʃendio]
disaster	disastro (m)	[di'zastro]
meteorite	meteorite (m)	[meteo'rite]

avalanche	valanga (f)	[va'langa]
snowslide	slavina (f)	[zla'vina]
blizzard	tempesta (f) di neve	[tem'pesta di 'neve]
snowstorm	bufera (f) di neve	['bufera di 'neve]

T&P BOOKS

FAUNA

T&P Books Publishing

predator	predatore (m)	[preda'tore]
tiger	tigre (f)	['tigre]
lion	leone (m)	[le'one]
wolf	lupo (m)	['lupo]
fox	volpe (m)	['volpe]

jaguar	giaguaro (m)	[dʒa'gwaro]
leopard	leopardo (m)	[leo'pardo]
cheetah	ghepardo (m)	[ge'pardo]

black panther	pantera (f)	[pan'tera]
puma	puma (f)	['puma]
snow leopard	leopardo (m) delle nevi	[leo'pardo 'delle 'nevi]
lynx	lince (f)	['lintʃe]

coyote	coyote (m)	[ko'jote]
jackal	sciacallo (m)	[ʃa'kallo]
hyena	iena (f)	['jena]

| animal | animale (m) | [ani'male] |
| beast (animal) | bestia (f) | ['bestia] |

squirrel	scoiattolo (m)	[sko'jattolo]
hedgehog	riccio (m)	['ritʃo]
hare	lepre (f)	['lepre]
rabbit	coniglio (m)	[ko'niʎʎo]

badger	tasso (m)	['tasso]
raccoon	procione (f)	[pro'tʃone]
hamster	criceto (m)	[kri'tʃeto]
marmot	marmotta (f)	[mar'motta]

mole	talpa (f)	['talpa]
mouse	topo (m)	['topo]
rat	ratto (m)	['ratto]
bat	pipistrello (m)	[pipi'strello]

ermine	ermellino (m)	[ermel'lino]
sable	zibellino (m)	[dzibel'lino]
marten	martora (f)	['martora]

| weasel | donnola (f) | ['donnola] |
| mink | visone (m) | [vi'zone] |

| beaver | castoro (m) | [kas'toro] |
| otter | lontra (f) | ['lontra] |

horse	cavallo (m)	[ka'vallo]
moose	alce (m)	['altʃe]
deer	cervo (m)	['tʃervo]
camel	cammello (m)	[kam'mello]

bison	bisonte (m) americano	[bi'zonte ameri'kano]
wisent	bisonte (m) europeo	[bi'zonte euro'peo]
buffalo	bufalo (m)	['bufalo]

zebra	zebra (f)	['dzebra]
antelope	antilope (f)	[an'tilope]
roe deer	capriolo (m)	[kapri'olo]
fallow deer	daino (m)	['daino]
chamois	camoscio (m)	[ka'moʃo]
wild boar	cinghiale (m)	[tʃin'gjale]

whale	balena (f)	[ba'lena]
seal	foca (f)	['foka]
walrus	tricheco (m)	[tri'keko]
fur seal	otaria (f)	[o'taria]
dolphin	delfino (m)	[del'fino]

bear	orso (m)	['orso]
polar bear	orso (m) bianco	['orso 'bjanko]
panda	panda (m)	['panda]

monkey	scimmia (f)	['ʃimmia]
chimpanzee	scimpanzè (m)	[ʃimpan'dze]
orangutan	orango (m)	[o'rango]
gorilla	gorilla (m)	[go'rilla]
macaque	macaco (m)	[ma'kako]
gibbon	gibbone (m)	[dʒib'bone]

| elephant | elefante (m) | [ele'fante] |
| rhinoceros | rinoceronte (m) | [rinotʃe'ronte] |

| giraffe | giraffa (f) | [dʒi'raffa] |
| hippopotamus | ippopotamo (m) | [ippo'potamo] |

| kangaroo | canguro (m) | [kan'guro] |
| koala (bear) | koala (m) | [ko'ala] |

mongoose	mangusta (f)	[man'gusta]
chinchilla	cincillà (f)	[tʃintʃil'la]
skunk	moffetta (f)	[mof'fetta]
porcupine	istrice (m)	['istritʃe]

89. Domestic animals

cat	gatta (f)	['gatta]
tomcat	gatto (m)	['gatto]
dog	cane (m)	['kane]
horse	cavallo (m)	[ka'vallo]
stallion (male horse)	stallone (m)	[stal'lone]
mare	giumenta (f)	[dʒu'menta]
cow	mucca (f)	['mukka]
bull	toro (m)	['toro]
ox	bue (m)	['bue]
sheep (ewe)	pecora (f)	['pekora]
ram	montone (m)	[mon'tone]
goat	capra (f)	['kapra]
billy goat, he-goat	caprone (m)	[kap'rone]
donkey	asino (m)	['azino]
mule	mulo (m)	['mulo]
pig, hog	porco (m)	['porko]
piglet	porcellino (m)	[portʃel'lino]
rabbit	coniglio (m)	[ko'niʎʎo]
hen (chicken)	gallina (f)	[gal'lina]
rooster	gallo (m)	['gallo]
duck	anatra (f)	['anatra]
drake	maschio (m) dell'anatra	['maskio dell 'anatra]
goose	oca (f)	['oka]
tom turkey, gobbler	tacchino (m)	[tak'kino]
turkey (hen)	tacchina (f)	[tak'kina]
domestic animals	animali (m pl) domestici	[ani'mali do'mestitʃi]
tame (e.g., ~ hamster)	addomesticato	[addomesti'kato]
to tame (vt)	addomesticare (vt)	[addomesti'kare]
to breed (vt)	allevare (vt)	[alle'vare]
farm	fattoria (f)	[fatto'ria]
poultry	pollame (m)	[pol'lame]
cattle	bestiame (m)	[bes'tjame]
herd (cattle)	branco (m), mandria (f)	['branko], ['mandria]
stable	scuderia (f)	[skude'ria]
pigpen	porcile (m)	[por'tʃile]
cowshed	stalla (f)	['stalla]
rabbit hutch	conigliera (f)	[koniʎ'ʎera]
hen house	pollaio (m)	[pol'lajo]

90. Birds

bird	uccello (m)	[u'tʃello]
pigeon	colombo (m), piccione (m)	[kolombo], [pi'tʃone]
sparrow	passero (m)	['passero]
tit (great tit)	cincia (f)	['tʃintʃa]
magpie	gazza (f)	['gattsa]
raven	corvo (m)	['korvo]
crow	cornacchia (f)	[kor'nakkia]
jackdaw	taccola (f)	['takkola]
rook	corvo (m) nero	['korvo 'nero]
duck	anatra (f)	['anatra]
goose	oca (f)	['oka]
pheasant	fagiano (m)	[fa'dʒano]
eagle	aquila (f)	['akwila]
hawk	astore (m)	[a'store]
falcon	falco (m)	['falko]
vulture	grifone (m)	[gri'fone]
condor (Andean ~)	condor (m)	['kondor]
swan	cigno (m)	['tʃiɲo]
crane	gru (f)	[gru]
stork	cicogna (f)	[tʃi'koɲa]
parrot	pappagallo (m)	[pappa'gallo]
hummingbird	colibrì (m)	[koli'bri]
peacock	pavone (m)	[pa'vone]
ostrich	struzzo (m)	['struttso]
heron	airone (m)	[ai'rone]
flamingo	fenicottero (m)	[feni'kottero]
pelican	pellicano (m)	[pelli'kano]
nightingale	usignolo (m)	[uzi'ɲolo]
swallow	rondine (f)	['rondine]
thrush	tordo (m)	['tordo]
song thrush	tordo (m) sasello	['tordo sa'zello]
blackbird	merlo (m)	['merlo]
swift	rondone (m)	[ron'done]
lark	allodola (f)	[al'lodola]
quail	quaglia (f)	['kwaʎʎa]
woodpecker	picchio (m)	['pikkio]
cuckoo	cuculo (m)	['kukulo]
owl	civetta (f)	[tʃi'vetta]

eagle owl	gufo (m) reale	['gufo re'ale]
wood grouse	urogallo (m)	[uro'gallo]
black grouse	fagiano (m) di monte	[fa'dʒano di 'monte]
partridge	pernice (f)	[per'nitʃe]

starling	storno (m)	['storno]
canary	canarino (m)	[kana'rino]
hazel grouse	francolino (m) di monte	[franko'lino di 'monte]
chaffinch	fringuello (m)	[frin'gwello]
bullfinch	ciuffolotto (m)	[tʃuffo'lotto]

seagull	gabbiano (m)	[gab'bjano]
albatross	albatro (m)	['albatro]
penguin	pinguino (m)	[pin'gwino]

91. Fish. Marine animals

bream	abramide (f)	[a'bramide]
carp	carpa (f)	['karpa]
perch	perca (f)	['perka]
catfish	pesce (m) gatto	['peʃe 'gatto]
pike	luccio (m)	['lutʃo]

salmon	salmone (m)	[sal'mone]
sturgeon	storione (m)	[sto'rjone]

herring	aringa (f)	[a'ringa]
Atlantic salmon	salmone (m)	[sal'mone]
mackerel	scombro (m)	['skombro]
flatfish	sogliola (f)	['soʎʎoʎa]

zander, pike perch	lucioperca (f)	[lutʃo'perka]
cod	merluzzo (m)	[mer'luttso]
tuna	tonno (m)	['tonno]
trout	trota (f)	['trota]

eel	anguilla (f)	[an'gwilla]
electric ray	torpedine (f)	[tor'pedine]
moray eel	murena (f)	[mu'rena]
piranha	piranha, piragna (f)	[pi'rania]

shark	squalo (m)	['skwalo]
dolphin	delfino (m)	[del'fino]
whale	balena (f)	[ba'lena]

crab	granchio (m)	['grankio]
jellyfish	medusa (f)	[me'duza]
octopus	polpo (m)	['polpo]
starfish	stella (f) marina	['stella ma'rina]
sea urchin	riccio (m) di mare	['ritʃo di 'mare]

seahorse	cavalluccio (m) marino	[kaval'lutʃo ma'rino]
oyster	ostrica (f)	['ostrika]
shrimp	gamberetto (m)	[gambe'retto]
lobster	astice (m)	['astitʃe]
spiny lobster	aragosta (f)	[ara'gosta]

92. Amphibians. Reptiles

snake	serpente (m)	[ser'pente]
venomous (snake)	velenoso	[vele'nozo]

viper	vipera (f)	['vipera]
cobra	cobra (m)	['kobra]
python	pitone (m)	[pi'tone]
boa	boa (m)	['boa]

grass snake	biscia (f)	['biʃa]
rattle snake	serpente (m) a sonagli	[ser'pente a so'naʎʎi]
anaconda	anaconda (f)	[ana'konda]

lizard	lucertola (f)	[lu'tʃertola]
iguana	iguana (f)	[i'gwana]
monitor lizard	varano (m)	[va'rano]
salamander	salamandra (f)	[sala'mandra]
chameleon	camaleonte (m)	[kamale'onte]
scorpion	scorpione (m)	[skor'pjone]

turtle	tartaruga (f)	[tarta'ruga]
frog	rana (f)	['rana]
toad	rospo (m)	['rospo]
crocodile	coccodrillo (m)	[kokko'drillo]

93. Insects

insect, bug	insetto (m)	[in'setto]
butterfly	farfalla (f)	[far'falla]
ant	formica (f)	[for'mika]
fly	mosca (f)	['moska]
mosquito	zanzara (f)	[dzan'dzara]
beetle	scarabeo (m)	[skara'beo]

wasp	vespa (f)	['vespa]
bee	ape (f)	['ape]
bumblebee	bombo (m)	['bombo]
gadfly (botfly)	tafano (m)	[ta'fano]

spider	ragno (m)	['raɲo]
spiderweb	ragnatela (f)	[raɲa'tela]

dragonfly	**libellula** (f)	[li'bellula]
grasshopper	**cavalletta** (f)	[kaval'letta]
moth (night butterfly)	**farfalla** (f) **notturna**	[far'falla not'turna]

cockroach	**scarafaggio** (m)	[skara'fadʒo]
tick	**zecca** (f)	['tsekka]
flea	**pulce** (f)	['pulʧe]
midge	**moscerino** (m)	[moʃe'rino]

locust	**locusta** (f)	[lo'kusta]
snail	**lumaca** (f)	[lu'maka]
cricket	**grillo** (m)	['grillo]
lightning bug	**lucciola** (f)	['luʧola]
ladybug	**coccinella** (f)	[koʧi'nella]
cockchafer	**maggiolino** (m)	[madʒo'lino]

leech	**sanguisuga** (f)	[sangwi'zuga]
caterpillar	**bruco** (m)	['bruko]
earthworm	**verme** (m)	['verme]
larva	**larva** (m)	['larva]

FLORA

T&P Books Publishing

94. Trees

tree	**albero** (m)	['albero]
deciduous (adj)	**deciduo**	[de'ʧiduo]
coniferous (adj)	**conifero**	[ko'nifero]
evergreen (adj)	**sempreverde**	[sempre'verde]
apple tree	**melo** (m)	['melo]
pear tree	**pero** (m)	['pero]
sweet cherry tree	**ciliegio** (m)	[ʧi'ljeʤo]
sour cherry tree	**amareno** (m)	[ama'reno]
plum tree	**prugno** (m)	['pruɲo]
birch	**betulla** (f)	[be'tulla]
oak	**quercia** (f)	['kwerʧa]
linden tree	**tiglio** (m)	['tiʎʎo]
aspen	**pioppo** (m) **tremolo**	['pjoppo 'tremolo]
maple	**acero** (m)	['aʧero]
spruce	**abete** (m)	[a'bete]
pine	**pino** (m)	['pino]
larch	**larice** (m)	['lariʧe]
fir tree	**abete** (m) **bianco**	[a'bete 'bjanko]
cedar	**cedro** (m)	['ʧedro]
poplar	**pioppo** (m)	['pjoppo]
rowan	**sorbo** (m)	['sorbo]
willow	**salice** (m)	['saliʧe]
alder	**alno** (m)	['alno]
beech	**faggio** (m)	['faʤo]
elm	**olmo** (m)	['olmo]
ash (tree)	**frassino** (m)	['frassino]
chestnut	**castagno** (m)	[ka'staɲo]
magnolia	**magnolia** (f)	[ma'ɲolia]
palm tree	**palma** (f)	['palma]
cypress	**cipresso** (m)	[ʧi'presso]
mangrove	**mangrovia** (f)	[man'growia]
baobab	**baobab** (m)	[bao'bab]
eucalyptus	**eucalipto** (m)	[ewka'lipto]
sequoia	**sequoia** (f)	[se'kwoja]

95. Shrubs

| bush | cespuglio (m) | [t͡ʃes'puʎʎo] |
| shrub | arbusto (m) | [ar'busto] |

| grapevine | vite (f) | ['vite] |
| vineyard | vigneto (m) | [vi'ɲeto] |

raspberry bush	lampone (m)	[lam'pone]
redcurrant bush	ribes (m) rosso	['ribes 'rosso]
gooseberry bush	uva (f) spina	['uva 'spina]

acacia	acacia (f)	[a'kat͡ʃa]
barberry	crespino (m)	[kres'pino]
jasmine	gelsomino (m)	[d͡ʒelso'mino]

juniper	ginepro (m)	[d͡ʒi'nepro]
rosebush	roseto (m)	[ro'zeto]
dog rose	rosa (f) canina	['roza ka'nina]

96. Fruits. Berries

fruit	frutto (m)	['frutto]
fruits	frutti (m pl)	['frutti]
apple	mela (f)	['mela]
pear	pera (f)	['pera]
plum	prugna (f)	['pruɲa]

strawberry (garden ~)	fragola (f)	['fragola]
sour cherry	amarena (f)	[ama'rena]
sweet cherry	ciliegia (f)	[t͡ʃi'ljed͡ʒa]
grape	uva (f)	['uva]

raspberry	lampone (m)	[lam'pone]
blackcurrant	ribes (m) nero	['ribes 'nero]
redcurrant	ribes (m) rosso	['ribes 'rosso]
gooseberry	uva (f) spina	['uva 'spina]
cranberry	mirtillo (m) di palude	[mir'tillo di pa'lude]

orange	arancia (f)	[a'rant͡ʃa]
mandarin	mandarino (m)	[manda'rino]
pineapple	ananas (m)	[ana'nas]
banana	banana (f)	[ba'nana]
date	dattero (m)	['dattero]

lemon	limone (m)	[li'mone]
apricot	albicocca (f)	[albi'kokka]
peach	pesca (f)	['peska]
kiwi	kiwi (m)	['kiwi]

grapefruit	pompelmo (m)	[pom'pelmo]
berry	bacca (f)	['bakka]
berries	bacche (f pl)	['bakke]
cowberry	mirtillo (m) rosso	[mir'tillo 'rosso]
wild strawberry	fragola (f) di bosco	['fragola di 'bosko]
bilberry	mirtillo (m)	[mir'tillo]

97. Flowers. Plants

flower	fiore (m)	['fjore]
bouquet (of flowers)	mazzo (m) di fiori	['mattso di 'fjori]
rose (flower)	rosa (f)	['roza]
tulip	tulipano (m)	[tuli'pano]
carnation	garofano (m)	[ga'rofano]
gladiolus	gladiolo (m)	[gla'djolo]
cornflower	fiordaliso (m)	[fjorda'lizo]
harebell	campanella (f)	[kampa'nella]
dandelion	soffione (m)	[sof'fjone]
camomile	camomilla (f)	[kamo'milla]
aloe	aloe (m)	['aloe]
cactus	cactus (m)	['kaktus]
rubber plant, ficus	ficus (m)	['fikus]
lily	giglio (m)	['dʒiʎʎo]
geranium	geranio (m)	[dʒe'ranio]
hyacinth	giacinto (m)	[dʒa'ʧinto]
mimosa	mimosa (f)	[mi'moza]
narcissus	narciso (m)	[nar'ʧizo]
nasturtium	nasturzio (m)	[na'sturtsio]
orchid	orchidea (f)	[orki'dea]
peony	peonia (f)	[pe'onia]
violet	viola (f)	[vi'ola]
pansy	viola (f) del pensiero	[vi'ola del pen'sjero]
forget-me-not	nontiscordardimè (m)	[non·ti·skordar·di'me]
daisy	margherita (f)	[marge'rita]
poppy	papavero (m)	[pa'pavero]
hemp	canapa (f)	['kanapa]
mint	menta (f)	['menta]
lily of the valley	mughetto (m)	[mu'getto]
snowdrop	bucaneve (m)	[buka'neve]
nettle	ortica (f)	[or'tika]
sorrel	acetosa (f)	[aʧe'toza]

water lily	ninfea (f)	[nin'fea]
fern	felce (f)	['feltʃe]
lichen	lichene (m)	[li'kene]

conservatory (greenhouse)	serra (f)	['serra]
lawn	prato (m) erboso	['prato er'bozo]
flowerbed	aiuola (f)	[aju'ola]

plant	pianta (f)	['pjanta]
grass	erba (f)	['erba]
blade of grass	filo (m) d'erba	['filo 'derba]

leaf	foglia (f)	['foʎʎa]
petal	petalo (m)	['petalo]
stem	stelo (m)	['stelo]
tuber	tubero (m)	['tubero]

| young plant (shoot) | germoglio (m) | [dʒer'moʎʎo] |
| thorn | spina (f) | ['spina] |

to blossom (vi)	fiorire (vi)	[fjo'rire]
to fade, to wither	appassire (vi)	[appas'sire]
smell (odor)	odore (m), profumo (m)	[o'dore], [pro'fumo]
to cut (flowers)	tagliare (vt)	[taʎ'ʎare]
to pick (a flower)	cogliere (vt)	['koʎʎere]

98. Cereals, grains

grain	grano (m)	['grano]
cereal crops	cereali (m pl)	[tʃere'ali]
ear (of barley, etc.)	spiga (f)	['spiga]

wheat	frumento (m)	[fru'mento]
rye	segale (f)	['segale]
oats	avena (f)	[a'vena]
millet	miglio (m)	['miʎʎo]
barley	orzo (m)	['ortso]

corn	mais (m)	['mais]
rice	riso (m)	['rizo]
buckwheat	grano (m) saraceno	['grano sara'tʃeno]

pea plant	pisello (m)	[pi'zello]
kidney bean	fagiolo (m)	[fa'dʒolo]
soy	soia (f)	['soja]
lentil	lenticchie (f pl)	[len'tikkje]
beans (pulse crops)	fave (f pl)	['fave]

T&P BOOKS

COUNTRIES OF
THE WORLD

T&P Books Publishing

Afghanistan	Afghanistan (m)	[af'ganistan]
Albania	Albania (f)	[alba'nia]
Argentina	Argentina (f)	[ardʒen'tina]
Armenia	Armenia (f)	[ar'menia]
Australia	Australia (f)	[au'stralia]
Austria	Austria (f)	['austria]
Azerbaijan	Azerbaigian (m)	[azerbaj'dʒan]
The Bahamas	le Bahamas	[le ba'amas]
Bangladesh	Bangladesh (m)	['bangladeʃ]
Belarus	Bielorussia (f)	[bjelo'russia]
Belgium	Belgio (m)	['beldʒo]
Bolivia	Bolivia (f)	[bo'livia]
Bosnia and Herzegovina	Bosnia-Erzegovina (f)	['boznia-ertse'govina]
Brazil	Brasile (m)	[bra'zile]
Bulgaria	Bulgaria (f)	[bulga'ria]
Cambodia	Cambogia (f)	[kam'bodʒa]
Canada	Canada (m)	['kanada]
Chile	Cile (m)	['tʃile]
China	Cina (f)	['tʃina]
Colombia	Colombia (f)	[ko'lombia]
Croatia	Croazia (f)	[kro'atsia]
Cuba	Cuba (f)	['kuba]
Cyprus	Cipro (m)	['tʃipro]
Czech Republic	Repubblica (f) Ceca	[re'pubblika 'tʃeka]
Denmark	Danimarca (f)	[dani'marka]
Dominican Republic	Repubblica (f) Dominicana	[re'pubblika domini'kana]
Ecuador	Ecuador (m)	[ekva'dor]
Egypt	Egitto (m)	[e'dʒitto]
England	Inghilterra (f)	[ingil'terra]
Estonia	Estonia (f)	[es'tonia]
Finland	Finlandia (f)	[fin'landia]
France	Francia (f)	['frantʃa]
French Polynesia	Polinesia (f) Francese	[poli'nezia fran'tʃeze]
Georgia	Georgia (f)	[dʒe'ordʒa]
Germany	Germania (f)	[dʒer'mania]
Ghana	Ghana (m)	['gana]
Great Britain	Gran Bretagna (f)	[gran bre'taɲa]
Greece	Grecia (f)	['gretʃa]
Haiti	Haiti (m)	[a'iti]
Hungary	Ungheria (f)	[unge'ria]

100. Countries. Part 2

Iceland	**Islanda** (f)	[iz'landa]
India	**India** (f)	['india]
Indonesia	**Indonesia** (f)	[indo'nezia]
Iran	**Iran** (m)	['iran]
Iraq	**Iraq** (m)	['irak]
Ireland	**Irlanda** (f)	[ir'landa]
Israel	**Israele** (m)	[izra'ele]
Italy	**Italia** (f)	[i'talia]
Jamaica	**Giamaica** (f)	[dʒa'majka]
Japan	**Giappone** (m)	[dʒap'pone]
Jordan	**Giordania** (f)	[dʒor'dania]
Kazakhstan	**Kazakistan** (m)	[ka'zakistan]
Kenya	**Kenya** (m)	['kenia]
Kirghizia	**Kirghizistan** (m)	[kir'gizistan]
Kuwait	**Kuwait** (m)	[ku'vejt]
Laos	**Laos** (m)	['laos]
Latvia	**Lettonia** (f)	[let'tonia]
Lebanon	**Libano** (m)	['libano]
Libya	**Libia** (f)	['libia]
Liechtenstein	**Liechtenstein** (m)	['liktenstajn]
Lithuania	**Lituania** (f)	[litu'ania]
Luxembourg	**Lussemburgo** (m)	[lussem'burgo]
Macedonia (Republic of ~)	**Macedonia** (f)	[matʃe'donia]
Madagascar	**Madagascar** (m)	[madagas'kar]
Malaysia	**Malesia** (f)	[ma'lezia]
Malta	**Malta** (f)	['malta]
Mexico	**Messico** (m)	['messiko]
Moldova, Moldavia	**Moldavia** (f)	[mol'davia]
Monaco	**Monaco** (m)	['monako]
Mongolia	**Mongolia** (f)	[mo'ngolia]
Montenegro	**Montenegro** (m)	[monte'negro]
Morocco	**Marocco** (m)	[ma'rokko]
Myanmar	**Birmania** (f)	[bir'mania]
Namibia	**Namibia** (f)	[na'mibia]
Nepal	**Nepal** (m)	[ne'pal]
Netherlands	**Paesi Bassi** (m pl)	[pa'ezi 'bassi]
New Zealand	**Nuova Zelanda** (f)	[nu'ova dze'landa]
North Korea	**Corea** (f) **del Nord**	[ko'rea del nord]
Norway	**Norvegia** (f)	[nor'vedʒa]

101. Countries. Part 3

Pakistan	**Pakistan** (m)	['pakistan]
Palestine	**Palestina** (f)	[pale'stina]

Panama	**Panama** (m)	['panama]
Paraguay	**Paraguay** (m)	[para'gwaj]
Peru	**Perù** (m)	[pe'ru]
Poland	**Polonia** (f)	[po'lonia]
Portugal	**Portogallo** (f)	[porto'gallo]
Romania	**Romania** (f)	[roma'nia]
Russia	**Russia** (f)	['russia]
Saudi Arabia	**Arabia Saudita** (f)	[a'rabia sau'dita]
Scotland	**Scozia** (f)	['skotsia]
Senegal	**Senegal** (m)	[sene'gal]
Serbia	**Serbia** (f)	['serbia]
Slovakia	**Slovacchia** (f)	[zlo'vakkia]
Slovenia	**Slovenia** (f)	[zlo'venia]
South Africa	**Repubblica** (f) **Sudafricana**	[re'pubblika sudafri'kana]
South Korea	**Corea** (f) **del Sud**	[ko'rea del sud]
Spain	**Spagna** (f)	['spaɲa]
Suriname	**Suriname** (m)	[suri'name]
Sweden	**Svezia** (f)	['zvetsia]
Switzerland	**Svizzera** (f)	['zvittsera]
Syria	**Siria** (f)	['siria]
Taiwan	**Taiwan** (m)	[taj'van]
Tajikistan	**Tagikistan** (m)	[ta'dʒikistan]
Tanzania	**Tanzania** (f)	[tan'dzania]
Tasmania	**Tasmania** (f)	[taz'mania]
Thailand	**Tailandia** (f)	[taj'landia]
Tunisia	**Tunisia** (f)	[tuni'zia]
Turkey	**Turchia** (f)	[tur'kia]
Turkmenistan	**Turkmenistan** (m)	[turk'menistan]
Ukraine	**Ucraina** (f)	[uk'raina]
United Arab Emirates	**Emirati** (m pl) **Arabi**	[emi'rati 'arabi]
United States of America	**Stati** (m pl) **Uniti d'America**	['stati u'niti da'merika]
Uruguay	**Uruguay** (m)	[uru'gwaj]
Uzbekistan	**Uzbekistan** (m)	[uz'bekistan]
Vatican	**Vaticano** (m)	[vati'kano]
Venezuela	**Venezuela** (f)	[venetsu'ela]
Vietnam	**Vietnam** (m)	['vjetnam]
Zanzibar	**Zanzibar**	['dzandzibar]

GASTRONOMIC GLOSSARY

This section contains a lot of words and terms associated with food. This dictionary will make it easier for you to understand the menu at a restaurant and choose the right dish

T&P Books Publishing

aftertaste	retrogusto (m)	[retro'gusto]
almond	mandorla (f)	['mandorla]
anise	anice (m)	['anitʃe]
aperitif	aperitivo (m)	[aperi'tivo]
appetite	appetito (m)	[appe'tito]
appetizer	antipasto (m)	[anti'pasto]
apple	mela (f)	['mela]
apricot	albicocca (f)	[albi'kokka]
artichoke	carciofo (m)	[kar'tʃofo]
asparagus	asparago (m)	[a'sparago]
Atlantic salmon	salmone (m)	[sal'mone]
avocado	avocado (m)	[avo'kado]
bacon	pancetta (f)	[pan'tʃetta]
banana	banana (f)	[ba'nana]
barley	orzo (m)	['ortso]
bartender	barista (m)	[ba'rista]
basil	basilico (m)	[ba'ziliko]
bay leaf	alloro (m)	[al'loro]
beans	fave (f pl)	['fave]
beef	manzo (m)	['mandzo]
beer	birra (f)	['birra]
beet	barbabietola (f)	[barba'bjetola]
bell pepper	peperone (m)	[pepe'rone]
berries	bacche (f pl)	['bakke]
berry	bacca (f)	['bakka]
bilberry	mirtillo (m)	[mir'tillo]
birch bolete	porcinello (m)	[portʃi'nello]
bitter	amaro	[a'maro]
black coffee	caffè (m) nero	[kaf'fe 'nero]
black pepper	pepe (m) nero	['pepe 'nero]
black tea	tè (m) nero	[te 'nero]
blackberry	mora (f)	['mora]
blackcurrant	ribes (m) nero	['ribes 'nero]
boiled	bollito	[bol'lito]
bottle opener	apribottiglie (m)	[apribot'tiʎʎe]
bread	pane (m)	['pane]
breakfast	colazione (f)	[kola'tsjone]
bream	abramide (f)	[a'bramide]
broccoli	broccolo (m)	['brokkolo]
Brussels sprouts	cavoletti (m pl) di Bruxelles	[kavo'letti di bruk'sel]
buckwheat	grano (m) saraceno	['grano sara'tʃeno]
butter	burro (m)	['burro]
buttercream	crema (f)	['krema]

cabbage	cavolo (m)	['kavolo]
cake	tortina (f)	[tor'tina]
cake	torta (f)	['torta]
calorie	caloria (f)	[kalo'ria]
can opener	apriscatole (m)	[apri'skatole]
candy	caramella (f)	[kara'mella]
canned food	cibi (m pl) in scatola	['tʃibi in 'skatola]
cappuccino	cappuccino (m)	[kappu'tʃino]
caraway	cumino, comino (m)	[ku'mino], [ko'mino]
carbohydrates	carboidrati (m pl)	[karboi'drati]
carbonated	gassata	[gas'sata]
carp	carpa (f)	['karpa]
carrot	carota (f)	[ka'rota]
catfish	pesce (m) gatto	['peʃe 'gatto]
cauliflower	cavolfiore (m)	[kavol'fjore]
caviar	caviale (m)	[ka'vjale]
celery	sedano (m)	['sedano]
cep	porcino (m)	[por'tʃino]
cereal crops	cereali (m pl)	[tʃere'ali]
champagne	champagne (m)	[ʃam'paɲ]
chanterelle	gallinaccio (m)	[galli'natʃo]
check	conto (m)	['konto]
cheese	formaggio (m)	[for'madʒo]
chewing gum	gomma (f) da masticare	['gomma da masti'kare]
chicken	pollo (m)	['pollo]
chocolate	cioccolato (m)	[tʃokko'lato]
chocolate	al cioccolato	[al tʃokko'lato]
cinnamon	cannella (f)	[kan'nella]
clear soup	brodo (m)	['brodo]
cloves	chiodi (m pl) di garofano	['kjodi di ga'rofano]
cocktail	cocktail (m)	['koktejl]
coconut	noce (f) di cocco	['notʃe di 'kokko]
cod	merluzzo (m)	[mer'luttso]
coffee	caffè (m)	[kaf'fe]
coffee with milk	caffè latte (m)	[kaf'fe 'latte]
cognac	cognac (m)	['koɲak]
cold	freddo	['freddo]
condensed milk	latte (m) condensato	['latte konden'sato]
condiment	condimento (m)	[kondi'mento]
confectionery	pasticceria (f)	[pastitʃe'ria]
cookies	biscotti (m pl)	[bi'skotti]
coriander	coriandolo (m)	[kori'andolo]
corkscrew	cavatappi (m)	[kava'tappi]
corn	mais (m)	['mais]
corn	mais (m)	['mais]
cornflakes	fiocchi (m pl) di mais	['fjokki di 'mais]
course, dish	piatto (m)	['pjatto]
cowberry	mirtillo (m) rosso	[mir'tillo 'rosso]
crab	granchio (m)	['graŋkio]
cranberry	mirtillo (m) di palude	[mir'tillo di pa'lude]
cream	panna (f)	['panna]
crumb	briciola (f)	['britʃola]

crustaceans	crostacei (m pl)	[kro'statʃei]
cucumber	cetriolo (m)	[tʃetri'olo]
cuisine	cucina (f)	[ku'tʃina]
cup	tazza (f)	['tattsa]
dark beer	birra (f) scura	['birra 'skura]
date	dattero (m)	['dattero]
death cap	fungo (m) moscario	['fungo mos'kario]
dessert	dolce (m)	['doltʃe]
diet	dieta (f)	[di'eta]
dill	aneto (m)	[a'neto]
dinner	cena (f)	['tʃena]
dried	secco	['sekko]
drinking water	acqua (f) potabile	['akwa po'tabile]
duck	anatra (f)	['anatra]
ear	spiga (f)	['spiga]
edible mushroom	fungo (m) commestibile	['fungo komme'stibile]
eel	anguilla (f)	[an'gwilla]
egg	uovo (m)	[u'ovo]
egg white	albume (m)	[al'bume]
egg yolk	tuorlo (m)	[tu'orlo]
eggplant	melanzana (f)	[melan'tsana]
eggs	uova (f pl)	[u'ova]
Enjoy your meal!	Buon appetito!	[bu'on appe'tito]
fats	grassi (m pl)	['grassi]
fig	fico (m)	['fiko]
filling	ripieno (m)	[ri'pjeno]
fish	pesce (m)	['peʃe]
flatfish	sogliola (f)	['soʎʎoʎa]
flour	farina (f)	[fa'rina]
fly agaric	ovolaccio (m)	[ovo'latʃo]
food	cibo (m)	['tʃibo]
fork	forchetta (f)	[for'ketta]
freshly squeezed juice	spremuta (f)	[spre'muta]
fried	fritto	['fritto]
fried eggs	uova (f pl) al tegamino	[u'ova al tega'mino]
frozen	congelato	[kondʒe'lato]
fruit	frutto (m)	['frutto]
fruits	frutti (m pl)	['frutti]
game	cacciagione (f)	[katʃa'dʒone]
gammon	prosciutto (m) affumicato	[pro'ʃutto affumi'kato]
garlic	aglio (m)	['aʎʎo]
gin	gin (m)	[dʒin]
ginger	zenzero (m)	['dzendzero]
glass	bicchiere (m)	[bik'kjere]
glass	calice (m)	['kalitʃe]
goose	oca (f)	['oka]
gooseberry	uva (f) spina	['uva 'spina]
grain	grano (m)	['grano]
grape	uva (f)	['uva]
grapefruit	pompelmo (m)	[pom'pelmo]
green tea	tè (m) verde	[te 'verde]
greens	verdura (f)	[ver'dura]

groats	cereali (m pl)	[tʃere'ali]
halibut	ippoglosso (m)	[ippo'glosso]
ham	prosciutto (m)	[pro'ʃutto]
hamburger	carne (f) trita	['karne 'trita]
hamburger	hamburger (m)	[am'burger]
hazelnut	nocciola (f)	[no'tʃola]
herring	aringa (f)	[a'ringa]
honey	miele (m)	['mjele]
horseradish	cren (m)	['kren]
hot	caldo	['kaldo]
ice	ghiaccio (m)	['gjatʃo]
ice-cream	gelato (m)	[dʒe'lato]
instant coffee	caffè (m) solubile	[kaf'fe so'lubile]
jam	marmellata (f)	[marmel'lata]
jam	marmellata (f)	[marmel'lata]
juice	succo (m)	['sukko]
kidney bean	fagiolo (m)	[fa'dʒolo]
kiwi	kiwi (m)	['kiwi]
knife	coltello (m)	[kol'tello]
lamb	agnello (m)	[a'ɲello]
lemon	limone (m)	[li'mone]
lemonade	limonata (f)	[limo'nata]
lentil	lenticchie (f pl)	[len'tikkje]
lettuce	lattuga (f)	[lat'tuga]
light beer	birra (f) chiara	['birra 'kjara]
liqueur	liquore (m)	[li'kwore]
liquors	bevande (f pl) alcoliche	[be'vande al'kolike]
liver	fegato (m)	['fegato]
lunch	pranzo (m)	['prantso]
mackerel	scombro (m)	['skombro]
mandarin	mandarino (m)	[manda'rino]
mango	mango (m)	['mango]
margarine	margarina (f)	[marga'rina]
marmalade	marmellata (f) di agrumi	[marmel'lata di a'grumi]
mashed potatoes	purè (m) di patate	[pu're di pa'tate]
mayonnaise	maionese (m)	[majo'neze]
meat	carne (f)	['karne]
melon	melone (m)	[me'lone]
menu	menù (m)	[me'nu]
milk	latte (m)	['latte]
milkshake	frullato (m)	[frul'lato]
millet	miglio (m)	['miʎʎo]
mineral water	acqua (f) minerale	['akwa mine'rale]
morel	spugnola (f)	['spuɲola]
mushroom	fungo (m)	['fungo]
mustard	senape (f)	[se'nape]
non-alcoholic	analcolico	[anal'koliko]
noodles	tagliatelle (f pl)	[taʎʎa'telle]
oats	avena (f)	[a'vena]
olive oil	olio (m) d'oliva	['oljo do'liva]
olives	olive (f pl)	[o'live]
omelet	frittata (f)	[frit'tata]

onion	cipolla (f)	[tʃi'polla]
orange	arancia (f)	[a'rantʃa]
orange juice	succo (m) d'arancia	['sukko da'rantʃa]
orange-cap boletus	boleto (m) rufo	[bo'leto 'rufo]
oyster	ostrica (f)	['ostrika]
pâté	pâté (m)	[pa'te]
papaya	papaia (f)	[pa'paja]
paprika	paprica (f)	['paprika]
parsley	prezzemolo (m)	[pret'tsemolo]
pasta	pasta (f)	['pasta]
pea	pisello (m)	[pi'zello]
peach	pesca (f)	['peska]
peanut	arachide (f)	[a'rakide]
pear	pera (f)	['pera]
peel	buccia (f)	['butʃa]
perch	perca (f)	['perka]
pickled	sottoaceto	[sottoa'tʃeto]
pie	crostata (f)	[kro'stata]
piece	pezzo (m)	['pettso]
pike	luccio (m)	['lutʃo]
pike perch	lucioperca (f)	[lutʃo'perka]
pineapple	ananas (m)	[ana'nas]
pistachios	pistacchi (m pl)	[pi'stakki]
pizza	pizza (f)	['pittsa]
plate	piatto (m)	['pjatto]
plum	prugna (f)	['pruɲa]
poisonous mushroom	fungo (m) velenoso	['fungo vele'nozo]
pomegranate	melagrana (f)	[mela'grana]
pork	maiale (m)	[ma'jale]
porridge	porridge (m)	[por'ridʒe]
portion	porzione (f)	[por'tsjone]
potato	patata (f)	[pa'tata]
proteins	proteine (f pl)	[prote'ine]
pub, bar	pub (m), bar (m)	[pab], [bar]
pudding	budino (m)	[bu'dino]
pumpkin	zucca (f)	['dzukka]
rabbit	coniglio (m)	[ko'niʎʎo]
radish	ravanello (m)	[rava'nello]
raisin	uvetta (f)	[u'vetta]
raspberry	lampone (m)	[lam'pone]
recipe	ricetta (f)	[ri'tʃetta]
red pepper	peperoncino (m)	[peperon'tʃino]
red wine	vino (m) rosso	['vino 'rosso]
redcurrant	ribes (m) rosso	['ribes 'rosso]
refreshing drink	bibita (f)	['bibita]
rice	riso (m)	['rizo]
rum	rum (m)	[rum]
russula	rossola (f)	['rossola]
rye	segale (f)	['segale]
saffron	zafferano (m)	[dzaffe'rano]
salad	insalata (f)	[insa'lata]
salmon	salmone (m)	[sal'mone]

salt	sale (m)	['sale]
salty	salato	[sa'lato]
sandwich	panino (m)	[pa'nino]
sardine	sardina (f)	[sar'dina]
sauce	salsa (f)	['salsa]
saucer	piattino (m)	[pjat'tino]
sausage	salame (m)	[sa'lame]
seafood	frutti (m pl) di mare	['frutti di 'mare]
sesame	sesamo (m)	[sezamo]
shark	squalo (m)	['skwalo]
shrimp	gamberetto (m)	[gambe'retto]
side dish	contorno (m)	[kon'torno]
slice	fetta (f), fettina (f)	['fetta], [fet'tina]
smoked	affumicato	[affumi'kato]
soft drink	bevanda (f) analcolica	[be'vanda anal'kolika]
soup	minestra (f)	[mi'nestra]
soup spoon	cucchiaio (m)	[kuk'kjajo]
sour cherry	amarena (f)	[ama'rena]
sour cream	panna (f) acida	['panna 'atʃida]
soy	soia (f)	['soja]
spaghetti	spaghetti (m pl)	[spa'getti]
sparkling	frizzante	[frid'dzante]
spice	spezie (f pl)	['spetsie]
spinach	spinaci (m pl)	[spi'natʃi]
spiny lobster	aragosta (f)	[ara'gosta]
spoon	cucchiaio (m)	[kuk'kjajo]
squid	calamaro (m)	[kala'maro]
steak	bistecca (f)	[bi'stekka]
still	liscia, non gassata	['liʃa], [non gas'sata]
strawberry	fragola (f)	['fragola]
sturgeon	storione (m)	[sto'rjone]
sugar	zucchero (m)	['dzukkero]
sunflower oil	olio (m) di girasole	['oljo di dʒira'sole]
sweet	dolce	['doltʃe]
sweet cherry	ciliegia (f)	[tʃi'ljedʒa]
taste, flavor	gusto (m)	['gusto]
tasty	buono, gustoso	[bu'ono], [gu'stozo]
tea	tè (m)	[te]
teaspoon	cucchiaino (m) da tè	[kuk'kjajno da 'te]
tip	mancia (f)	['mantʃa]
tomato	pomodoro (m)	[pomo'doro]
tomato juice	succo (m) di pomodoro	['sukko di pomo'doro]
tongue	lingua (f)	['lingua]
toothpick	stuzzicadenti (m)	[stuttsika'denti]
trout	trota (f)	['trota]
tuna	tonno (m)	['tonno]
turkey	tacchino (m)	[tak'kino]
turnip	rapa (f)	['rapa]
veal	vitello (m)	[vi'tello]
vegetable oil	olio (m) vegetale	['oljo vedʒe'tale]
vegetables	ortaggi (m pl)	[or'tadʒi]
vegetarian	vegetariano (m)	[vedʒeta'rjano]

vegetarian	**vegetariano**	[vedʒeta'rjano]
vermouth	**vermouth** (m)	['vermut]
vienna sausage	**würstel** (m)	['vyrstel]
vinegar	**aceto** (m)	[a'tʃeto]
vitamin	**vitamina** (f)	[vita'mina]
vodka	**vodka** (f)	['vodka]
wafers	**wafer** (m)	['vafer]
waiter	**cameriere** (m)	[kame'rjere]
waitress	**cameriera** (f)	[kame'rjera]
walnut	**noce** (f)	['notʃe]
water	**acqua** (f)	['akwa]
watermelon	**anguria** (f)	[an'guria]
wheat	**frumento** (m)	[fru'mento]
whiskey	**whisky**	['wiski]
white wine	**vino** (m) **bianco**	['vino 'bjanko]
wild strawberry	**fragola** (f) **di bosco**	['fragola di 'bosko]
wine	**vino** (m)	['vino]
wine list	**lista** (f) **dei vini**	['lista 'dei 'vini]
with ice	**con ghiaccio**	[kon 'gjatʃo]
yogurt	**yogurt** (m)	['jogurt]
zucchini	**zucchina** (f)	[dzuk'kina]

Italian-English gastronomic glossary

abramide (f)	[a'bramide]	bream
aceto (m)	[a'tʃeto]	vinegar
acqua (f)	['akwa]	water
acqua (f) minerale	['akwa mine'rale]	mineral water
acqua (f) potabile	['akwa po'tabile]	drinking water
affumicato	[affumi'kato]	smoked
aglio (m)	['aʎʎo]	garlic
agnello (m)	[a'ɲello]	lamb
al cioccolato	[al tʃokko'lato]	chocolate
albicocca (f)	[albi'kokka]	apricot
albume (m)	[al'bume]	egg white
alloro (m)	[al'loro]	bay leaf
amarena (f)	[ama'rena]	sour cherry
amaro	[a'maro]	bitter
analcolico	[anal'koliko]	non-alcoholic
ananas (m)	[ana'nas]	pineapple
anatra (f)	['anatra]	duck
aneto (m)	[a'neto]	dill
anguilla (f)	[an'gwilla]	eel
anguria (f)	[an'guria]	watermelon
anice (m)	['anitʃe]	anise
antipasto (m)	[anti'pasto]	appetizer
aperitivo (m)	[aperi'tivo]	aperitif
appetito (m)	[appe'tito]	appetite
apribottiglie (m)	[apribot'tiʎʎe]	bottle opener
apriscatole (m)	[apri'skatole]	can opener
arachide (f)	[a'rakide]	peanut
aragosta (f)	[ara'gosta]	spiny lobster
arancia (f)	[a'rantʃa]	orange
aringa (f)	[a'ringa]	herring
asparago (m)	[a'sparago]	asparagus
avena (f)	[a'vena]	oats
avocado (m)	[avo'kado]	avocado
bacca (f)	['bakka]	berry
bacche (f pl)	['bakke]	berries
banana (f)	[ba'nana]	banana
barbabietola (f)	[barba'bjetola]	beet
barista (m)	[ba'rista]	bartender
basilico (m)	[ba'ziliko]	basil
bevanda (f) analcolica	[be'vanda anal'kolika]	soft drink
bevande (f pl) alcoliche	[be'vande al'kolike]	liquors
bibita (f)	['bibita]	refreshing drink
bicchiere (m)	[bik'kjere]	glass
birra (f)	['birra]	beer

birra (f) chiara	['birra 'kjara]	light beer
birra (f) scura	['birra 'skura]	dark beer
biscotti (m pl)	[bi'skotti]	cookies
bistecca (f)	[bi'stekka]	steak
boleto (m) rufo	[bo'leto 'rufo]	orange-cap boletus
bollito	[bol'lito]	boiled
briciola (f)	['britʃola]	crumb
broccolo (m)	['brokkolo]	broccoli
brodo (m)	['brodo]	clear soup
buccia (f)	['butʃa]	peel
budino (m)	[bu'dino]	pudding
Buon appetito!	[bu'on appe'tito]	Enjoy your meal!
buono, gustoso	[bu'ono], [gu'stozo]	tasty
burro (m)	['burro]	butter
cacciagione (f)	[katʃa'dʒone]	game
caffè (m)	[kaf'fe]	coffee
caffè (m) nero	[kaf'fe 'nero]	black coffee
caffè (m) solubile	[kaf'fe so'lubile]	instant coffee
caffè latte (m)	[kaf'fe 'latte]	coffee with milk
calamaro (m)	[kala'maro]	squid
caldo	['kaldo]	hot
calice (m)	['kalitʃe]	glass
caloria (f)	[kalo'ria]	calorie
cameriera (f)	[kame'rjera]	waitress
cameriere (m)	[kame'rjere]	waiter
cannella (f)	[kan'nella]	cinnamon
cappuccino (m)	[kappu'tʃino]	cappuccino
caramella (f)	[kara'mella]	candy
carboidrati (m pl)	[karboi'drati]	carbohydrates
carciofo (m)	[kar'tʃofo]	artichoke
carne (f)	['karne]	meat
carne (f) trita	['karne 'trita]	hamburger
carota (f)	[ka'rota]	carrot
carpa (f)	['karpa]	carp
cavatappi (m)	[kava'tappi]	corkscrew
caviale (m)	[ka'vjale]	caviar
cavoletti (m pl) di Bruxelles	[kavo'letti di bruk'sel]	Brussels sprouts
cavolfiore (m)	[kavol'fjore]	cauliflower
cavolo (m)	['kavolo]	cabbage
cena (f)	['tʃena]	dinner
cereali (m pl)	[tʃere'ali]	groats
cereali (m pl)	[tʃere'ali]	cereal crops
cetriolo (m)	[tʃetri'olo]	cucumber
champagne (m)	[ʃam'paɲ]	champagne
chiodi (m pl) di garofano	['kjodi di ga'rofano]	cloves
cibi (m pl) in scatola	['tʃibi in 'skatola]	canned food
cibo (m)	['tʃibo]	food
ciliegia (f)	[tʃi'ljedʒa]	sweet cherry
cioccolato (m)	[tʃokko'lato]	chocolate
cipolla (f)	[tʃi'polla]	onion
cocktail (m)	['koktejl]	cocktail

cognac (m)	['koɲak]	cognac
colazione (f)	[kola'tsjone]	breakfast
coltello (m)	[kol'tello]	knife
con ghiaccio	[kon 'gjatʃo]	with ice
condimento (m)	[kondi'mento]	condiment
congelato	[kondʒe'lato]	frozen
coniglio (m)	[ko'niʎʎo]	rabbit
conto (m)	['konto]	check
contorno (m)	[kon'torno]	side dish
coriandolo (m)	[kori'andolo]	coriander
crema (f)	['krema]	buttercream
cren (m)	['kren]	horseradish
crostacei (m pl)	[kro'statʃei]	crustaceans
crostata (f)	[kro'stata]	pie
cucchiaino (m) da tè	[kuk'kjajno da 'te]	teaspoon
cucchiaio (m)	[kuk'kjajo]	spoon
cucchiaio (m)	[kuk'kjajo]	soup spoon
cucina (f)	[ku'tʃina]	cuisine
cumino, comino (m)	[ku'mino], [ko'mino]	caraway
dattero (m)	['dattero]	date
dieta (f)	[di'eta]	diet
dolce	['doltʃe]	sweet
dolce (m)	['doltʃe]	dessert
fagiolo (m)	[fa'dʒolo]	kidney bean
farina (f)	[fa'rina]	flour
fave (f pl)	['fave]	beans
fegato (m)	['fegato]	liver
fetta (f), fettina (f)	['fetta], [fet'tina]	slice
fico (m)	['fiko]	fig
fiocchi (m pl) di mais	['fjokki di 'mais]	cornflakes
forchetta (f)	[for'ketta]	fork
formaggio (m)	[for'maddʒo]	cheese
fragola (f)	['fragola]	strawberry
fragola (f) di bosco	['fragola di 'bosko]	wild strawberry
freddo	['freddo]	cold
frittata (f)	[frit'tata]	omelet
fritto	['fritto]	fried
frizzante	[frid'dzante]	sparkling
frullato (m)	[frul'lato]	milkshake
frumento (m)	[fru'mento]	wheat
frutti (m pl)	['frutti]	fruits
frutti (m pl) di mare	['frutti di 'mare]	seafood
frutto (m)	['frutto]	fruit
fungo (m)	['fungo]	mushroom
fungo (m) commestibile	['fungo komme'stibile]	edible mushroom
fungo (m) moscario	['fungo mos'kario]	death cap
fungo (m) velenoso	['fungo vele'nozo]	poisonous mushroom
gallinaccio (m)	[galli'natʃo]	chanterelle
gamberetto (m)	[gambe'retto]	shrimp
gassata	[gas'sata]	carbonated
gelato (m)	[dʒe'lato]	ice-cream
ghiaccio (m)	['gjatʃo]	ice

gin (m)	[dʒin]	gin
gomma (f) da masticare	['gomma da masti'kare]	chewing gum
granchio (m)	['graŋkio]	crab
grano (m)	['grano]	grain
grano (m) saraceno	['grano sara'tʃeno]	buckwheat
grassi (m pl)	['grassi]	fats
gusto (m)	['gusto]	taste, flavor
hamburger (m)	[am'burger]	hamburger
insalata (f)	[insa'lata]	salad
ippoglosso (m)	[ippo'glosso]	halibut
kiwi (m)	['kiwi]	kiwi
lampone (m)	[lam'pone]	raspberry
latte (m)	['latte]	milk
latte (m) condensato	['latte konden'sato]	condensed milk
lattuga (f)	[lat'tuga]	lettuce
lenticchie (f pl)	[len'tikkje]	lentil
limonata (f)	[limo'nata]	lemonade
limone (m)	[li'mone]	lemon
lingua (f)	['lingua]	tongue
liquore (m)	[li'kwore]	liqueur
liscia, non gassata	['liʃa], [non gas'sata]	still
lista (f) dei vini	['lista 'dei 'vini]	wine list
luccio (m)	['lutʃo]	pike
lucioperca (f)	[lutʃo'perka]	pike perch
maiale (m)	[ma'jale]	pork
maionese (m)	[majo'neze]	mayonnaise
mais (m)	['mais]	corn
mais (m)	['mais]	corn
mancia (f)	['mantʃa]	tip
mandarino (m)	[manda'rino]	mandarin
mandorla (f)	['mandorla]	almond
mango (m)	['mango]	mango
manzo (m)	['mandzo]	beef
margarina (f)	[marga'rina]	margarine
marmellata (f)	[marmel'lata]	jam
marmellata (f)	[marmel'lata]	jam
marmellata (f) di agrumi	[marmel'lata di a'grumi]	marmalade
mela (f)	['mela]	apple
melagrana (f)	[mela'grana]	pomegranate
melanzana (f)	[melan'tsana]	eggplant
melone (m)	[me'lone]	melon
menù (m)	[me'nu]	menu
merluzzo (m)	[mer'luttso]	cod
miele (m)	['mjele]	honey
miglio (m)	['miʎʎo]	millet
minestra (f)	[mi'nestra]	soup
mirtillo (m)	[mir'tillo]	bilberry
mirtillo (m) di palude	[mir'tillo di pa'lude]	cranberry
mirtillo (m) rosso	[mir'tillo 'rosso]	cowberry
mora (f)	['mora]	blackberry
nocciola (f)	[no'tʃola]	hazelnut
noce (f)	['notʃe]	walnut

noce (f) di cocco	['notʃe di 'kokko]	coconut
oca (f)	['oka]	goose
olio (m) d'oliva	['oljo do'liva]	olive oil
olio (m) di girasole	['oljo di dʒira'sole]	sunflower oil
olio (m) vegetale	['oljo vedʒe'tale]	vegetable oil
olive (f pl)	[o'live]	olives
ortaggi (m pl)	[or'tadʒi]	vegetables
orzo (m)	['ortso]	barley
ostrica (f)	['ostrika]	oyster
ovolaccio (m)	[ovo'latʃo]	fly agaric
pâté (m)	[pa'te]	pâté
pancetta (f)	[pan'tʃetta]	bacon
pane (m)	['pane]	bread
panino (m)	[pa'nino]	sandwich
panna (f)	['panna]	cream
panna (f) acida	['panna 'atʃida]	sour cream
papaia (f)	[pa'paja]	papaya
paprica (f)	['paprika]	paprika
pasta (f)	['pasta]	pasta
pasticceria (f)	[pastitʃe'ria]	confectionery
patata (f)	[pa'tata]	potato
pepe (m) nero	['pepe 'nero]	black pepper
peperoncino (m)	[peperon'tʃino]	red pepper
peperone (m)	[pepe'rone]	bell pepper
pera (f)	['pera]	pear
perca (f)	['perka]	perch
pesca (f)	['peska]	peach
pesce (m)	['peʃe]	fish
pesce (m) gatto	['peʃe 'gatto]	catfish
pezzo (m)	['pettso]	piece
piattino (m)	[pjat'tino]	saucer
piatto (m)	['pjatto]	course, dish
piatto (m)	['pjatto]	plate
pisello (m)	[pi'zello]	pea
pistacchi (m pl)	[pi'stakki]	pistachios
pizza (f)	['pittsa]	pizza
pollo (m)	['pollo]	chicken
pomodoro (m)	[pomo'doro]	tomato
pompelmo (m)	[pom'pelmo]	grapefruit
porcinello (m)	[portʃi'nello]	birch bolete
porcino (m)	[por'tʃino]	cep
porridge (m)	[por'ridʒe]	porridge
porzione (f)	[por'tsjone]	portion
pranzo (m)	['prantso]	lunch
prezzemolo (m)	[pret'tsemolo]	parsley
prosciutto (m)	[pro'ʃutto]	ham
prosciutto (m) affumicato	[pro'ʃutto affumi'kato]	gammon
proteine (f pl)	[prote'ine]	proteins
prugna (f)	['pruɲa]	plum
pub (m), bar (m)	[pab], [bar]	pub, bar
purè (m) di patate	[pu're di pa'tate]	mashed potatoes
rapa (f)	['rapa]	turnip

ravanello (m)	[rava'nello]	radish
retrogusto (m)	[retro'gusto]	aftertaste
ribes (m) nero	['ribes 'nero]	blackcurrant
ribes (m) rosso	['ribes 'rosso]	redcurrant
ricetta (f)	[ri'tʃetta]	recipe
ripieno (m)	[ri'pjeno]	filling
riso (m)	['rizo]	rice
rossola (f)	['rossola]	russula
rum (m)	[rum]	rum
salame (m)	[sa'lame]	sausage
salato	[sa'lato]	salty
sale (m)	['sale]	salt
salmone (m)	[sal'mone]	salmon
salmone (m)	[sal'mone]	Atlantic salmon
salsa (f)	['salsa]	sauce
sardina (f)	[sar'dina]	sardine
scombro (m)	['skombro]	mackerel
secco	['sekko]	dried
sedano (m)	['sedano]	celery
segale (f)	['segale]	rye
senape (f)	[se'nape]	mustard
sesamo (m)	[sezamo]	sesame
sogliola (f)	['soʎʎoʎa]	flatfish
soia (f)	['soja]	soy
sottoaceto	[sottoa'tʃeto]	pickled
spaghetti (m pl)	[spa'getti]	spaghetti
spezie (f pl)	['spetsie]	spice
spiga (f)	['spiga]	ear
spinaci (m pl)	[spi'natʃi]	spinach
spremuta (f)	[spre'muta]	freshly squeezed juice
spugnola (f)	['spuɲola]	morel
squalo (m)	['skwalo]	shark
storione (m)	[sto'rjone]	sturgeon
stuzzicadenti (m)	[stuttsika'denti]	toothpick
succo (m)	['sukko]	juice
succo (m) d'arancia	['sukko da'rantʃa]	orange juice
succo (m) di pomodoro	['sukko di pomo'doro]	tomato juice
tè (m)	[te]	tea
tè (m) nero	[te 'nero]	black tea
tè (m) verde	[te 'verde]	green tea
tacchino (m)	[tak'kino]	turkey
tagliatelle (f pl)	[taʎʎa'telle]	noodles
tazza (f)	['tattsa]	cup
tonno (m)	['tonno]	tuna
torta (f)	['torta]	cake
tortina (f)	[tor'tina]	cake
trota (f)	['trota]	trout
tuorlo (m)	[tu'orlo]	egg yolk
uova (f pl)	[u'ova]	eggs
uova (f pl) al tegamino	[u'ova al tega'mino]	fried eggs
uovo (m)	[u'ovo]	egg
uva (f)	['uva]	grape

uva (f) **spina**	['uva 'spina]	gooseberry
uvetta (f)	[u'vetta]	raisin
vegetariano	[vedʒeta'rjano]	vegetarian
vegetariano (m)	[vedʒeta'rjano]	vegetarian
verdura (f)	[ver'dura]	greens
vermouth (m)	['vermut]	vermouth
vino (m)	['vino]	wine
vino (m) **bianco**	['vino 'bjanko]	white wine
vino (m) **rosso**	['vino 'rosso]	red wine
vitamina (f)	[vita'mina]	vitamin
vitello (m)	[vi'tello]	veal
vodka (f)	['vodka]	vodka
würstel (m)	['vyrstel]	vienna sausage
wafer (m)	['vafer]	wafers
whisky	['wiski]	whiskey
yogurt (m)	['jogurt]	yogurt
zafferano (m)	[dzaffe'rano]	saffron
zenzero (m)	['dzendzero]	ginger
zucca (f)	['dzukka]	pumpkin
zucchero (m)	['dzukkero]	sugar
zucchina (f)	[dzuk'kina]	zucchini

www.ingramcontent.com/pod-product-compliance
Lightning Source LLC
LaVergne TN
LVHW051731080426
835511LV00018B/2998